THE THEOLOGY OF THE BOOK OF JEREMIAH

The Book of Jeremiah, second of the three major prophets, is immensely complex. Its different interpretive voices stretch across several generations and do not cohere into an easily identifiable and uniform theology. Instead, in both poetry and prose, the Book of Jeremiah witnesses an ongoing conversation among different advocates concerning the crisis of Babylon's expansion and Jerusalem's demise. In this volume, Walter Brueggemann elucidates these various voices in the context of Judah's commitment to the rule of the one God, YHWH. This messy interface of the theological and political constitutes the primal challenge of the Book of Jeremiah, and Brueggemann shows how the book asserts that God continues to be similarly and disturbingly operative in the affairs of the world. In this way, contemporary crises such as American imperialism and religiously inspired terrorism are shown to be dislocations with ancient antecedents, but dislocations that continue to invite readers to new futures that combine divine agency and human inventiveness rooted in faithfulness.

Walter Brueggemann is William Marcellus McPheeters Professor Emeritus of Old Testament at Columbia Theological Seminary. Although his impact on the study of much of the biblical canon is widespread, he is probably best known for his scholarship on the Psalms and prophetic literature. His many books include *An Introduction to the Old Testament: The Canon and Christian Imagination* and *Theology of the Old Testament: Testimony, Dispute, Advocacy*, and he will co-author, with William H. Bellinger, Jr., the two-volume *New Cambridge Bible Commentary on the Psalms*.

OLD TESTAMENT THEOLOGY

GENERAL EDITORS

Brent A. Strawn,
Assistant Professor of Old Testament Theology,
Candler School of Theology

Patrick D. Miller,
Charles T. Haley Professor of Old Testament Theology,
Princeton Theological Seminary

This series aims to remedy the deficiency of available published material on the theological concerns of the Old Testament books. Here, specialists explore the theological richness of a given book at greater length than is usually possible in the introductions to commentaries or as part of other Old Testament theologies. They are also able to investigate the theological themes and issues of their chosen books without being tied to a commentary format or to a thematic structure provided from elsewhere. When complete, the series will cover all the Old Testament writings and will thus provide an attractive, and timely, range of short texts around which courses can be developed.

FORTHCOMING VOLUMES

The Theology of the Book of Genesis, R. Walter L. Moberly

The Theology of the Book of Leviticus, Brent A. Strawn

The Theology of the Book of Judges, Joel S. Kaminsky

The Theology of the Book of Psalms, Patrick D. Miller

The Theology of the Book of Ecclesiastes, J. Gerald Janzen

The Theology of the Book of Daniel, Anathea Portier-Young

The Theology of the Book of Hosea, Christine Roy Yoder

The Theology of the Book of Amos, John Barton

In grateful memory

of

Shirley C. Guthrie

❧

THE THEOLOGY OF THE
BOOK OF JEREMIAH

WALTER BRUEGGEMANN

Columbia Theological Seminary

CAMBRIDGE UNIVERSITY PRESS
Cambridge, New York, Melbourne, Madrid, Cape Town, Singapore, São Paulo

Cambridge University Press
32 Avenue of the Americas, New York, NY 10013-2473, USA

www.cambridge.org
Information on this title: www.cambridge.org/9780521844543

First published 2007

Printed in the United States of America

A catalog record for this publication is available from the British Library.

Library of Congress Cataloging in Publication Data

Brueggemann, Walter.
The theology of the book of Jeremiah / Walter Brueggemann.
p.   cm. – (Old Testament theology)
Includes bibliographical references (p.   ) and index.
ISBN 0-521-84454-1 (hardback) – ISBN 0-521-60629-2 (pbk.)
1. Bible. O.T. Jeremiah – Theology.   I. Title.   II. Series.
BS1525.52.B79   2007
224′.206–dc22   2006014946

ISBN-13   978-0-521-84454-3 hardback
ISBN-10   0-521-84454-1 hardback

ISBN-13   978-0-521-60629-5 paperback
ISBN-10   0-521-60629-2 paperback

Contents

General Editors' Preface

Some years ago, Cambridge University Press, under the editorship of James D. G. Dunn, initiated a series entitled *New Testament Theology*. The first volumes appeared in 1991 and the series was brought to completion in 2003. For whatever reason, a companion series that would focus on the Old Testament/Hebrew Bible was never planned or executed. The present series, *Old Testament Theology*, is intended to rectify this need.

The reasons delineated by Dunn that justified the publication of *New Testament Theology* continue to hold true for *Old Testament Theology*. These include, among other things, the facts that, (1) given faculty and curricular structures in many schools, the theological study of individual Old Testament writings is often spotty at best; (2) most exegetical approaches (and commentaries) proceed verse by verse so that theological interests are in competition with, if not completely eclipsed by, other important issues, whether historical, grammatical, or literary; and (3) commentaries often confine their discussion of a book's theology to just a few pages in the introduction. The dearth of materials focused exclusively on a particular book's theology may be seen as a result of factors like these; or, perhaps, it is the cause of such factors. Regardless, as Dunn concluded, without adequate theological resources there is little incentive for teachers or students to engage the theology of specific books; they must be content with what are mostly general overviews. Perhaps the most serious problem resulting from all this is that students are at a disadvantage, even incapacitated, when it comes to the matter of integrating their study of the Bible with other courses in religion and theology. There is, therefore, an urgent need for a series to bridge the gap between the too-slim theological précis and the too-full commentary where theological concerns are lost among many others.

All of these factors commend the publication of *Old Testament Theology* now, just as they did for *New Testament Theology* more than a decade ago. Like its sister series, *Old Testament Theology* is a place where Old Testament scholars can write at greater length on the theology of individual biblical books and may do so without being tied to the linear, verse-by-verse format of the commentary genre or a thematic structure of some sort imposed on the text from outside. Each volume in the series seeks to describe the biblical book's theology as well as to engage the book theologically – that is, each volume intends to *do* theology through and with the biblical book under discussion, as well as delineate the theology contained within it. Among other things, theological engagement with the composition includes paying attention to its contribution to the canon and appraising its influence on and reception by later communities of faith. In these ways, *Old Testament Theology* seeks to emulate its New Testament counterpart.

In the intervening years since *New Testament Theology* was first conceived, however, developments have taken place in the field that provide still further reasons for the existence of *Old Testament Theology*; these have impact on how the series is envisioned and implemented and also serve to distinguish it, however slightly, from its companion series. Three developments in particular are noteworthy:

1. *The present hermeneutical climate,* often identified (rightly or wrongly) as "postmodern," is rife with possibility and potential for new ways of theologizing about Scripture and its constituent parts. Theologizing in this new climate will of necessity look (and be) different from how it has ever looked (or been) before.

2. *There has been an ethos change in the study of religion, broadly, and in biblical studies in particular.* No longer are the leading scholars in the field only Christian clergy, whether Catholic priests or mainline Protestant ministers. Jewish scholars and scholars of other Christian traditions are every bit as prominent, as are scholars of the non- or even anti-confessional stripe. In short, now is a time when "Old Testament Theology" must be conducted without the benefits of many of the old consensuses and certainties, even the most basic ones relating to epistemological framework and agreed-upon interpretative communities along with their respective traditions.

3. Finally, recent years have witnessed *a long-overdue rapprochement among biblical scholars, ethicists, and systematic theologians.* Interdisciplinary studies between these groups are now regularly published, thus furthering and facilitating the need for books that make the theology of Scripture widely available for diverse publics.

In brief, the time is ripe for a series of books that will engage the theology of specific books of the Old Testament in a new climate for a new day. The result will not be programmatic, settled, or altogether certain. Despite that – or, in some ways, *because* of that – it is hoped that *Old Testament Theology* will contain highly useful volumes that are ideally poised to make significant contributions on a number of fronts including: (a) the ongoing discussion of biblical theology in confessional and nonconfessional mode as well as in postmodern and canonical contexts; (b) the theological exchange between Old Testament scholars and those working in cognate and disparate disciplines; and (c) the always pressing task of introducing students to the theology of the discrete canonical unit: the biblical books themselves.

Brent A. Strawn
Emory University

Patrick D. Miller
Princeton Theological Seminary

Preface

My study of Jeremiah goes back to ancient days, to my study with Lionel A. Whiston, Jr., at Eden Theological Seminary and with James Muilenburg at Union Theological Seminary. Since that time, I have been privileged to be in mostly friendly and always generative conversations with the principal interpreters of Jeremiah in our present generation: Robert P. Carroll, Ronald E. Clements, Terence E. Fretheim, William L. Holladay, Patrick D. Miller, Kathleen M. O'Connor, and Louis Stulman. (I heard Abraham Heschel lecture in only one series, and that concerned Jeremiah.) The present book reflects my engagement with these several writings in a way that has clarified and situated my own scholarship.

My point of reference for Jeremiah studies has been my teacher, James Muilenburg. He was among the most important Jeremiah scholars of his generation, although in the end he refused to let his commentary reach publication. Muilenburg's attention to rhetorical detail has largely dictated my method, and his passion for the prophetic tradition leads me to see in powerful ways the interface of the text with the issues that face our own culture in a time of "plucking up and tearing down." I am blessed to be rooted in his teaching and to have been sent beyond his teaching in freedom.

I am glad to thank Patrick D. Miller and Brent A. Strawn for including me in the series and especially thank Brent for engaging me along the way with the manuscript. I am also particularly grateful to Tia Foley, who, like Baruch, has the skills that permit me to "add many words" and bring this manuscript to completion. I give my thanks to Chris Hooker for his preparation of the indexes. The biblical text has in it no indication of emphases for reading. In a number of texts quoted herein, I have italicized certain words in order to assist the reader in noting the rhetorical force of the text. In each case such underscoring is my own work and of course coheres with my own sense of the text.

I am pleased to dedicate this book to the memory of my colleague Shirley C. Guthrie. He and I were in good conversation over these issues over a long period of time. In the final days of his life up to his illness and death, he was reading my Jeremiah commentary and was both appreciative and critical in a way that let our conversation go further. I am glad to offer this memorial tribute to him in celebration of his gentle disputatiousness, his carefully honed cynical humor, and his deep faithfulness on the big issues. Such a force and such a presence he has been among us, and I stand among the great company of those grateful for him.

Walter Brueggemann
Columbia Theological Seminary

Abbreviations

AB	Anchor Bible
BibOr	Biblica et orientalia
BIS	Biblical Interpretation Series
BLS	Bible and Literature Series
BS	The Biblical Seminar
BZAW	Beihefte zur Zeitschrift für die alttestamentliche Wissenschaft
CBQ	*Catholic Biblical Quarterly*
ConBOT	Coniectanea biblica: Old Testament Series
HBT	*Horizons in Biblical Theology*
HSM	Harvard Semitic Monographs
ICC	International Critical Commentary
Interp	Interpretation: A Bible Commentary for Teaching and Preaching
IRT	Issues in Religion and Theology
JBL	*Journal of Biblical Literature*
JNES	*Journal of Near Eastern Studies*
JSOT	*Journal for the Study of the Old Testament*
JSOTSup	Journal for the Study of the Old Testament Supplement Series

KHC	Kurzer Hand-Commentar zum Alten Testament
LAI	Library of Ancient Israel
LXX	Septuagint
MT	Masoretic Text
NRSV	New Revised Standard Version
OBT	Overtures to Biblical Theology
OTL	Old Testament Library
PTMS	Pittsburgh Theological Monograph Series
SBLDS	Society of Biblical Literature Dissertation Series
SBLMS	Society of Biblical Literature Monograph Series
SBLSymS	Society of Biblical Literature Symposium Series
SBT	Studies in Biblical Theology
SSN	Studia semitica neerlandica
ThSt	Theologische Studiën
ThTo	*Theology Today*
USQR	*Union Seminary Quarterly Review*
VT	*Vetus Testamentum*
VTSup	Supplements to Vetus Testamentum
WBC	Word Biblical Commentary
WW	*Word and World*
ZAW	*Zeitschrift für die alttestamentliche Wissenschaft*

CHAPTER 1

Critical Access to the Book of Jeremiah

The Book of Jeremiah, who was the second of the three major prophets, is situated between Isaiah and Ezekiel and is an immensely complex book. Indeed, it is so complex that some informed readers have concluded that it is impossible to read the book as a coherent whole and have declared it "unreadable." Although it is possible to see how different subsections of the book function and what they mean, it is not readily apparent how the subsections meaningfully fit together. This is but the first of several critical issues confronting any interpretation of the theology of the Book of Jeremiah.

COMPLEXITY AND CONTEXT

I identify two reasons for the book's complexity. First, the Book of Jeremiah consists of the swirling of several interpretive voices, each of which offers a strong reading of the historical–theological crisis that preoccupies the book. These several voices, moreover, are in some contestation with each other about the meaning and significance of the crisis of Jerusalem and about an appropriate response to that crisis. The traditioning process that produced the final form of the text, moreover, has made no noticeable efforts to adjudicate between or to bring together in a coherent manner those several contesting voices. Rather, the final form of the text has permitted the several contesting voices to stand alongside one another without noticeable harmonization.

In addition to the multiplicity of interpretive voices in the book, it is clear that the Book of Jeremiah is problematic because it stretches over several generations, certainly beyond the credible extent of the lifetime of the person of Jeremiah. Thus we see that the traditions of Jeremiah – no doubt rooted in *the person of Jeremiah* and eventuating in the final form of *the Book of Jeremiah* – are immensely generative; as a result, the dynamism of the tradition kept producing more words and eventually more texts, so that the book grew with "many similar words" (see Jer 36:32).

Thus the Book of Jeremiah evidences *many voices over time* that *do not readily cohere.* These several voices represent those who are in quite different historical circumstances, variously prior to the destruction of Jerusalem, in the wake of destruction, or at the cusp of restoration. They differ, however, not only because of different circumstances but also because they are rooted in different interpretive traditions, each of which perceived events differently.

The conventional critical resolution of the complexity of the Book of Jeremiah, attributed to Sigmund Mowinckel and Bernhard Duhm, is to posit three "sources," each of which has a share in the book.[1] The primary source, dubbed by these scholars source "A," consists of the assumed *words of Jeremiah*, characteristically

---

[1] This era of scholarship is given a brief review in Otto Eissfeldt, "The Prophetic Literature," in *The Old Testament and Modern Study: A Generation of Discovery and Research*, ed. H. H. Rowley (Oxford: Clarendon, 1951), 151–53. For Mowinckel and Duhm's works, see Sigmund Mowinckel, *Zur Komposition des Buches Jeremia* (Kristiania: J. Dybwad, 1914); and Bernhard Duhm, *Das Buch Jeremia*, KHC 11 (Tübingen: J. C. B. Mohr [P. Siebeck], 1901).

articulated in *poetic form*. The second source, dubbed "B," consists of texts – *mostly prose* – that are assigned to *Baruch*, Jeremiah's faithful secretary. Although this source of late has received little attention and has perhaps been explained away in more recent criticism, it was earlier thought at the outset to concern especially the narrative report of chapters 37–44, culminating in a prophetic oracle addressed to Baruch in chapter 45. Aside from the personal citation of Baruch, we may take "Baruch" as a metaphor for the emerging influence of "scribes."[2] The scribes were "book men" who produced scrolls that preserved earlier traditions and who thereby transposed prophetic utterances into a written form that eventually would become "Scripture."

The third source, "C," refers to *prose materials* – often *speeches* – that seem reminiscent of the cadences and theological perspective of the Book of Deuteronomy and so are termed *Deuteronomic* or *Deuteronomistic.* Whereas the poetry (in source A) seems to be poignantly addressed to a quite particular moment, the prose that is Deuteronomic takes a larger, nearly systemic view of matters and understands an occasion of prophetic utterance in a larger interpretive context. There can be no doubt of these distinctions in the Book of Jeremiah, even if we are not sure about their relationship to one another. Although contemporary scholars would prefer not to speak of "sources" as did our predecessors, there is no doubt that the "source analysis" did address the issue of coherence in a most complex text. The most acute critical question of the book is how to understand the relationships of these several voices with each other. We may notice three operative hypotheses.

---

[2] See Richard Elliot Friedman, *Who Wrote the Bible?* (New York: Harper and Row, 1987), 146–49, for a suggestive and somewhat quixotic judgment about the scribal process of making the Bible.

First, William L. Holladay, who has published the most extensive and detailed commentary on Jeremiah in recent times, takes
a critically conservative view and understands the poetry and the
prose to be intimately connected to each other, with all of it bearing
the stamp of the personality of the prophet.[3] Thus, as scholars have
sorted out what is "authentic" for the prophet, Holladay judges
most of the material as "genuine." At the present time, Holladay
represents a view that is out of fashion among interpreters.

Second, at the other extreme from Holladay is Robert P. Carroll, a most generative scholar in Jeremiah studies. Carroll tends
to discount what we may know or recover of the prophet himself.[4]
He judges that the Deuteronomic material is a weighty interpretive
imposition on whatever there was initially of poetry, so that the
prose material is now decisive and dominant and is to be understood as the primary intentionality of the final form of the book.
The consequence of Carroll's approach is to minimize interest in
the person of the prophet, to see the function of the book somewhat later, and to recognize that the book is a powerful ideological
statement that makes ready use of the legacy of the prophet, to
which we no longer have any direct access.

A third approach, by Louis Stulman, proposes that the prose
materials, mostly offered in large blocks of text, are strategically
placed in the editorial process to produce the canonical book.[5]
Those blocks are intended to function as interpretive reference

[3] William L. Holladay, *Jeremiah 1: A Commentary on the Book of the Prophet
Jeremiah Chapters 1–25*, Hermeneia (Philadelphia: Fortress, 1986), and *Jeremiah
2: A Commentary on the Book of the Prophet Jeremiah Chapters 26–52*,
Hermeneia (Philadelphia: Fortress, 1989).
[4] Robert P. Carroll, *Jeremiah*, OTL (Philadelphia: Westminster, 1986).
[5] Louis Stulman, *Order Amid Chaos: Jeremiah as Symbolic Tapestry*, BS 57
(Sheffield: Sheffield Academic Press, 1998).

points and clues for how the poetic materials around are to be read. Thus Stulman's approach is resonant with Carroll's accent on the prose. Unlike Carroll, however, Stulman does not believe that the prose passages constitute a distorting imposition on the poetry but rather function as a way to guide the reader through its complexity.

In any case, we may observe that interpreters now are not as inclined as in earlier generations to conjure distinctive "literary sources." Rather, we may think of these several distinct perspectives within the book as *crucial interpretive voices* in the community that insisted on a hearing and that, for whatever reason, were given a hearing in the final form of the text.[6] A move from "source" to "voice" permits us to understand the variety and tension in the book as a part of its organic coherence, albeit a quite complex coherence. Thus the book is not a scissors-and-paste job but rather an ongoing conversation among zealous advocates concerning the crisis faced by the community of Israel at the demise of Jerusalem.

The material that constitutes the Book of Jeremiah, with its several voices bespeaking different interpretive angles and vested interests, is completely geared toward the crisis of 587 BCE and the demise of Jerusalem.[7] The Book of Jeremiah arises from and reflects on the termination of the Davidic dynasty after four hundred years and on the destruction of the Temple of Solomon after its long run of dominance and legitimacy. The state of Israel, long presided over by the House of David, was a remarkable experiment in the ancient Near East, for not only was it a state committed to a single

---

[6] See Christopher R. Seitz, *Theology in Conflict: Reactions to the Exile in the Book of Jeremiah*, BZAW 176 (Berlin: de Gruyter, 1989).

[7] See Daniel L. Smith, *The Religion of the Landless: The Social Context of the Babylonian Exile* (Bloomington, IN: Meyer-Stone, 1989).

God, Yhwh, but, more importantly, the state claimed continuity with an older remembered tradition of covenant that antedated the state and that stood in some tension with the state. Because of that antecedent tradition of covenant, the monarchy and its capital city of Jerusalem were by definition at some odds with the geopolitical reality of the ancient Near East.[8] Consequently, this small, vulnerable state with its peculiar self-understanding had to exist amid the great powers of the region, Egypt to the south and several successive kingdoms to the north.

But the Book of Jeremiah emerges not only in the face of the crisis in Jerusalem. The Jerusalem crisis turned out to be an epitome of a larger upheaval in ancient Near Eastern geopolitics. Just prior to the destruction of the city of Jerusalem, the expansionist state of Assyria – long-standing and brutal – had disappeared from the map and had been promptly displaced by one of its established colonies, Babylon. The latter immediately became as expansionist as Assyria and so extended its political–military reach toward Jerusalem. After repeated incursions, the city of Jerusalem was finally taken by the Babylonians (see 2 Kings 24:10–25:21). It was, moreover, the policy of Babylon, as it had been of Assyria before, to deport the leading members of captured societies in order to minimize ongoing trouble among the conquered peoples (see 2 Kings 17:24–28). Thus, after the destruction of 587 BCE, the leading voices of Jerusalemite society, the ones who finally produced the Book of Jeremiah, were deported from Judah.

All of this political–military development is completely understandable in terms of conventional military operations and imperial treatment of conquered states. In Judah, however, in the

---

[8] See the theological exposition of the theme and the ensuing tensions in Martin Buber, *Kingship of God*, 3rd ed. (London: Humanities Press International, 1967).

environment of Jeremiah, the great crisis could not be adequately understood simply as a geopolitical event. The reason it could not be so treated is because Judah was, at least in principle, completely committed to the rule of the one God, Yhwh.[9] This one God, Yhwh, moreover, was known and said to be the God of covenant, who issued commandments and who enacted sanctions (blessings and curses) on those who did or did not keep those commandments. Because of this remarkable theological conviction about the rule of Yhwh, which extended into the public domain, it was inescapable that the crisis of Jerusalem would be interpreted in theological–covenantal categories. It is this that evokes the material that became the Book of Jeremiah, a multivoiced effort to make *theological sense* out of a *geopolitical crisis*. The effect of this interface of theological and military–political categories is the awareness that the crisis is to be understood in covenantal–moral categories and not just as the Realpolitik; it was instead a working out of the will of Yhwh, who is said to be, in the end, the ruler and arbiter of the entire public process of international politics.

Thus the "rise and fall" of the great powers is to be placed in the purview of Yhwh's rule.[10] Judah is not only the interpreter of that

[9] See Klaus Koch, *The Prophets I: The Assyrian Period* (Philadelphia: Fortress, 1983), 5 and passim, for his thesis of "metahistory" as a modern way of expressing what the prophets present as the rule of Yhwh.

[10] Elsewhere (Walter Brueggemann, *The Land: Place as Gift, Promise, and Challenge in Biblical Faith*, 2nd ed., OBT [Minneapolis: Fortress, 2002], xvii and n. 18), I have suggested that a contemporary, secular form of the same argument about the rule of Yhwh in the public process is offered by Paul M. Kennedy, *The Rise and Fall of the Great Powers: Economic Change and Military Conflict From 1500 to 2000* (New York: Random House, 1987). Kennedy's precise analysis, without reference to the rule of God, manifests that there are inexorable limits to the power of a nation-state that cannot be transgressed with impunity. The same argument is made by the prophets, only with explicit reference to the rule of Yhwh.

interface of YHWH and the public process but also a participant (perpetrator and/or victim) of this odd rule that defies conventional categories. This interface of the theological and the political constitutes the primal challenge of the Book of Jeremiah. It is surely a challenge to the modern reader who does not easily imagine such a defining theological agency in world affairs. In a different way, the same resistance to this interface must have been a challenge in the generic religious culture of the ancient Near East, for the insistence on the singular rule of YHWH over the nations was no less problematic in an ancient environment of religious pluralism than it is in a contemporary environment of secularism.

The stretch of the Book of Jeremiah over several generations emerges because this literature is devoted to a meditation on and interpretation of the crisis of Jerusalem, which was razed at the hands of the Babylonians.[11] It is conventional to assume that the tradition begins with the call of the prophet Jeremiah, perhaps in 621 BCE, at the time of the Reform of Josiah (see Jer 11; 2 Kings 22–23). But even if that date is a beginning point, it is the death of King Josiah in 609 BCE that seems to be a primary reference point in the book. Either way, the Book of Jeremiah contains much reflection that is situated before the destruction of Jerusalem in 587 BCE and offers anticipatory reflection on that pending loss. The tradition of Jeremiah is clearly familiar with the unimpressive kings who came after Josiah in Jerusalem, his three sons, and his grandson (see 2 Kings 23:31–25:7).

The Book of Jeremiah does not, however, end with the report on the destruction of Jerusalem in 587 BCE. It continues reflection on

---

[11] To this end, William McKane, in his *A Critical and Exegetical Commentary on Jeremiah*, 2 vols., ICC (Edinburgh: T. and T. Clark, 1986–1996), 1:1, has usefully termed the process a "rolling corpus."

the circumstances and faith of those who, after 587, were deported by the Babylonians into alien lands.[12] Thus, a second wave of reflection seems to arise from the community of the deported (see Jer 24), even though the text is well versed on the future Babylonian governor of the province, Gedaliah, after the catastrophe of 587 (Jer 40:7–41:18).[13] The Jeremian tradition offers reflection concerning both the sorry circumstances of those left in the land and the lives of those who were deported. For this period, then, the tradition offers quite a wide-angle view of the lives of those who suffered the loss of Jerusalem. It is clear, however, that the loss and dismay of deportation and demise is not the final word of the Book of Jeremiah. The tradition continues to be generative into the sixth century BCE, long enough that it may hope for and point to signs of recovery and restoration after the disaster.[14] Thus, the book offers a powerful statement of hope that would have been impossible for the person of Jeremiah himself. In the end, the book anticipates the destruction of "the Destroyer," Babylon, as the vindication of YHWH and as an expectation of restoration for the Jews (Jer 50–51; cf. Ps 137).[15] How much of that hope is singularly grounded in confidence in YHWH's

---

[12] See Daniel L. Smith-Christopher, *A Biblical Theology of Exile*, OBT (Minneapolis: Fortress, 2002).

[13] While the voice of those who remained in the land is thought to be heard in the Book of Lamentations, on the whole, the ideology of the exiles has crowded out such voices. See Norman K. Gottwald, "Social Class and Ideology in Isaiah 40–55: An Eagletonian Reading," in *The Bible and Liberation: Political and Social Hermeneutics*, ed. Norman K. Gottwald and Richard A. Horsley, rev. ed. (Maryknoll, NY: Orbis, 1993), 329–42.

[14] See Walter Brueggemann, "An Ending that Does Not End: The Book of Jeremiah," in *Postmodern Interpretations of the Bible: A Reader*, ed. A. K. M. Adam (St. Louis, MO: Chalice, 2001), 117–28.

[15] On this text, see Martin Kessler, *Battle of the Gods: The God of Israel Versus Marduk of Babylon – A Literary/Theological Interpretation of Jeremiah 50–51*, SSN 42 (Assen: Van Gorcum, 2003).

coming rule and how much of it is a comment on emerging geopolitical reality is difficult to determine. Either way, the dynamism of
the tradition makes possible a ringing affirmation, even in the face
of debilitating historical circumstances.

ROOTAGE

Neither the Book of Jeremiah nor the person of Jeremiah appeared
amid Jerusalem's climactic crisis de novo. Behind the person and the
book is a long tradition of faith that goes back to the very origins
of Israel as the people of Yhwh. We may identify three defining
moments in the tradition that are antecedent to the formation of
the Jeremian tradition.

First, at its deepest level the tradition of Jeremiah is rooted in the
memory and authority of the covenant at Sinai. There are immense
unsolvable problems connected with the Sinai tradition concerning its date, provenance, and character. Frank Crüsemann is perhaps most helpful in his judgment that, as a theological claim in
Israel, the covenant at Sinai stands outside time as an unqualified,
unconditioned absolute, whatever may be the historical matters
connected with it:

> Sinai is, however, a utopian place. It is temporally and physically
> outside state authority. The association of divine law with this place is
> completed by steps, which the catastrophe of Israel both enabled and
> compelled. Sinai became the fulcrum of a legal system not connected
> with the power of a state and therefore not a mere expression of
> tradition and custom. . . . The very real survival of Israel, in spite of
> the kind of conquest that had destroyed other nations, depends on a
> fictional place in an invented past. They escaped every earthly power
> and therefore are put ahead of those kingdoms.[16]

---

[16] Frank Crüsemann, *The Torah: Theology and Social History of Old Testament
Law* (Edinburgh: T. and T. Clark, 1996), 57.

Taken theologically, the awesome meeting at Mt. Sinai concerns the exclusive, uncompromising, nonnegotiable connection of Israel to YHWH. It is no longer possible to situate the Sinai covenant in the Late Bronze Age in relationship to the Hittite political treaties, as had been the case in mid-twentieth-century critical study. Nonetheless, that phase of scholarship – which now appears somewhat dated – helped to accentuate aspects of the meeting at Sinai, a meeting we here treat as a *canonical* rather than a *historical* reality.

It is clear that YHWH is the decisive and defining character in the meeting, who, at the same time, asserts a *cosmic sovereignty* and a *special commitment to Israel*:

> Now therefore, if you obey my voice and keep my covenant, you shall be my treasured possession out of all the peoples. Indeed, the whole earth is mine. (Exod 19:5)

This claim of sovereignty for YHWH is pervasive in the tradition of Sinai, evidenced especially in the theophanic report of Exodus 19:16–25 that witnesses to the awesome, even cataclysmic, coming of the person of YHWH.

That sovereignty, however, is not simply a brusque, one-dimensional assertion of power. It is rather a sovereignty that willingly participates in the public process of history in order to evoke, form, and commit to a new community that is constituted by the gathering of emancipated slaves:[17]

> I am the LORD your God, who brought you out of the land of Egypt, out of the house of slavery. (Exod 20:2)

That sovereign, now publicly engaged on behalf of Israel, issues a "policy statement" of divine requirements and expectations to which Israel must adhere. Thus the Ten Commandments explicate

---

[17] See Buber, *Kingship of God*, especially chapter 8.

the way in which YHWH intends the world and enunciates the pattern of conduct expected of this newly formed community (see Exod 20:3–17). It is usual to regard the first commandment as most defining of the relationship. In Exodus 20:3, the exclusive claim of YHWH on Israel is tersely voiced. Indeed, Henning Graf Reventlow can suggest that verse 3 is not a command but rather a statement of reality: there will not be other gods![18] The second commandment of Exodus 20:4–6 enunciates a characteristic theme of YHWH's aniconic character, a reality that precludes YHWH from being domesticated, confined, or robbed of freedom.

This fiercely demanding agenda will be, in the time to come, the defining substance of the covenantal relationship. It is, of course, to be noted that the commands are stated in an absolute form that simply refuses to entertain a thought of disobedience. Beyond that absolute tone, one may find in Exodus 23:20–33 the articulation, in inchoate form, of the covenantal sanctions that later became important in prophetic tradition. What begins inchoately becomes, later on, a full inventory of *divine blessings* in response to obedience and *divine curses* in response to disobedience (Lev 26; Deut 28). This paragraph in Exodus 23 is for the most part positive; it assumes obedience that will issue in success and prosperity. In verses 21 and 33, however, one can see the negative outcomes that will become greater in this unfolding tradition.

The culmination of this dramatic meeting at Sinai is found in Exodus 24:3–8, in which Israel twice pledges singular obedience to the commands of YHWH that have just been enunciated:

> Moses came and told the people all the words of the LORD and all the ordinances; and all the people answered with one voice, and said,

---

[18] Henning Graf Reventlow, *Gebot und Predigt im Dekalogue* (Gütersloh: G. Mohn, 1962), 25–28.

"All the words that the LORD has spoken we will do." (Exod 24:3; see also v. 7)

In fact, in the completed tradition, Israel had already signed on for full compliance with YHWH's will, even before the stipulations had been declared:

The people all answered as one: "Everything that the LORD has spoken we will do." (Exod 19:8)

Thus Israel's very character and historical existence, according to this tradition, are based on obedient attentiveness to YHWH and a readiness to be connected only to YHWH. The warning of Exodus 23:32–33 concerning "no other gods" and "no other covenants" is the most characteristic claim of this tradition.

When we speak of "covenant," it is clear that the defining mark of covenant is exactly and precisely *obedience to the Torah*. The Torah is enunciated in the most authoritative list of the Ten Commandments. It is clear nonetheless that the Torah that voices the divine will to which Israel is exclusively pledged has an immense dynamism to it, so that the initial declaration of the Ten Commandments is richly augmented, developed, and interpreted over time.[19] In the end, the "Sinai Covenant" includes the entire corpus of Exodus 25:1 through Numbers 10:10, plus the earlier law offered in Exodus 21:1–23:19. Clearly, YHWH's will for Israel extends to every detailed aspect of life. All of these detailed aspects of life, however, are in the service of the one central command of exclusive loyalty to YHWH. It is, so the tradition makes clear, the intent of YHWH to fashion a "holy people," a people whose life is totally congruent with the character of YHWH:

But you shall be for me a priestly kingdom. (Exod 19:6a)

---

[19] See Crüsemann, *The Torah*, especially chapter 3.

The motif of "holiness" is to mark Israel as distinct in the world; that insistence on holiness is given a particular form of interpretation in the "holiness traditions" of the priestly trajectory.[20] It is clear that Israel from the outset is to be radically different from every other historical people, is to rely only on YHWH for security, prosperity, and well-being, and is thus to refuse any alternative form of security, prosperity, or well-being that may be offered in a variety of cultural contexts.

Given the "absolute character" of this relationship with this nonnegotiable sovereign, we may take special note of Exodus 32–34, a part of the oldest tradition of Sinai.[21] In this narrative account, Israel violates the covenant so decisively that the tablets containing the commands are broken in an act signifying the end of the covenant (Exod 32:19). Given the absolute, nonnegotiable character of the covenant, we might expect this to be the final word on the relationship.

It is most surprising, then, in Exodus 33–34 to witness Moses, the great human agent and mediator of the covenant, negotiating with this nonnegotiable sovereign. In the end, the shrewd and demanding work of Moses permits YHWH to reconstitute the covenant with Israel on the grounds of YHWH's own mercy:

> He said: I hereby make a covenant. Before all your people I will perform marvels, such as have not been performed in all the earth or in any nation; and all the people among whom you live shall see the work of the LORD; for it is an awesome thing that I will do with you. (Exod 34:10)

---

[20] On the intense notions of holiness in the priestly traditions, see Crüsemann, *The Torah*, 277–327; and John G. Gammie, *Holiness in Israel*, OBT (Minneapolis: Fortress, 1989), 45–70.

[21] On this text, see R. W. L. Moberly, *At the Mountain of God: Story and Theology in Exodus 32–34*, JSOTSup 22 (Sheffield: JSOT Press, 1983).

This narrative deployment from Exodus 32 through Exodus 34 is exceedingly important because it attests that the covenant between exclusive sovereign and chosen people is not one-dimensional. Rather, the relationship is one of dynamism that permits the dramatic process of *covenant breaking* and *covenant making*. It is probable, moreover, that in Israel's developed liturgical practice, the Sinai covenant constituted a pattern of worship whereby wayward Israel returned – over and over – to obedience. This demanding sovereign – over and over – welcomed a wayward people back to the covenant (see, e.g., Ps 50, 81, 95). This dynamism in liturgical practice will be important as we consider the dramatic practices that are on exhibit in the tradition of Jeremiah.

Second, the more proximate source lying behind the tradition of Jeremiah is commonly thought to be the prophet Hosea.[22] Hosea, a northern prophet in the eighth century BCE, is thoroughly rooted, as Robert R. Wilson has shown, in an old and deep "Ephraimite tradition."[23] While Hosea seems to be immersed in and faithful to that tradition, it is equally clear that the tradition of Hosea exhibits remarkable innovation that will subsequently be taken up by Jeremiah. Most spectacularly, Hosea articulates the covenant of Sinai in terms of deep interpersonal imagery of marriage, divorce, and remarriage. While the personal experience of the prophet is often given considerable attention in scholarship, the more important gain, in this judgment, is Hosea's daring capacity to extend this imagery to Israel's covenant with YHWH. This interpretative memory, now casting covenant in interpersonal categories, keeps

[22] The classic study of the dependence of Jeremiah on the tradition of Hosea is by K. Gross, *Die literarische Verwandtschaft Jeremias mit Hosea* (Leipzig: Robert Noske, 1930), 1–19.

[23] Robert R. Wilson, *Prophecy and Society in Ancient Israel* (Philadelphia: Fortress, 1980), 226–51.

the covenant from being a mere formal transaction and marks it instead by pathos and pain, deep infidelity and betrayal, and the capacity for newness. The prize articulation of this act of prophetic imagination is the long poem of Hosea 2:2–23, a poem that David J. A. Clines has shown has remarkable artistic symmetry.[24] In verses 2–13, the wounded, betrayed, angry husband YHWH terminates the marriage with fickle Israel. In these verses, albeit cast in patriarchal rhetoric, YHWH is presented as a demanding sovereign. The poem turns, however, in verses 14–15 to evidence YHWH's pathos-filled yearning for reattachment to Israel, a yearning that becomes a full renewal of the relationship in verses 16–23. The sweep of this poetry is breathtaking; it voices the rich complexity of the covenant and the daring vulnerability of YHWH, who adjudicates between YHWH's own righteous wrath and YHWH's most elemental yearning for relatedness. This capacity of YHWH, as given to us by the poet, is paralleled in the remarkable poem of Hosea 11:1 –9, wherein YHWH again moves from anger to seeking love that makes newness possible. This poetic articulation positions the covenant of Sinai in a radically new and different way.

Having seen the large format of Hosea's utterance, we may mention a series of matters that will be important as we move toward our consideration of Jeremiah.

The Book of Hosea is saturated with covenant references. The most explicit reference to the commands of Sinai is in 4:2, a clear allusion to the Decalogue:

> Swearing, lying, and murder,
> and stealing and adultery break out;
> bloodshed follows bloodshed. (Hos 4:2)

---

[24]David J. A. Clines, "Hosea 2: Structure and Interpretation," in *Studia Biblica 1978: Old Testament and Related Themes*, ed. Elizabeth A. Livingstone, JSOTSup 11 (Sheffield: JSOT Press, 1978), 83–103.

Quite clearly, this prophet, faithful to Sinai, understood Israel to be under the absolute command of Yʜᴡʜ.

The sovereignty of Yʜᴡʜ over Israel – and over the nations and over creation – is everywhere in evidence in this tradition. In particular, two texts link the uncompromising sovereignty of Yʜᴡʜ to the Exodus, as it is articulated in the Sinai commands themselves:

> I am the Lᴏʀᴅ your God from the land of Egypt;
> I will make you live in tents again,
> as in the days of the appointed festival. (Hos 12:9)

* * *

> Yet I have been the Lᴏʀᴅ your God
> ever since the land of Egypt;
> you know no God but me,
> and besides me there is no savior. (Hos 13:4)

The tradition of Hosea offers what may be the only clear case in the prophets in which kings in principle are disapproved. In most places, kingship is assumed and indicted only for disobedience:

> They made kings, but not through me;
> they set up princes, but without my knowledge.
> With their silver and gold they made idols
> for their own destruction. (Hos 8:4)

Because the tradition of Jeremiah will expend extensive energy on the trouble wrought by kings, this harsh prophetic dismissal of kingship looms large in the background of Jeremiah. Although Hosea lacks a corpus of "Oracles Against the Nations" that occur in most pre-exilic prophets (and notably in Jer 46–51), the prophetic critique of covenantal failure in Israel is matched by reference to Assyria as a proximate agent of Yʜᴡʜ in working judgment against

Israel and Judah.[25] The references to Assyria in Hosea exhibit the way the prophets articulate the concrete rule of Y_HWH among the nations, a motif that will be crucial in Jeremiah. Twice in Hosea, Israel is condemned for "going to Assyria" and seeking help through an alliance:

> Ephraim has become like a dove,
> silly and without sense;
> they call upon Egypt, they go to Assyria. (Hos 7:11; see also 8:9)

Twice more, Assyria is an instrument of Y_HWH whereby Israel will be punished for its waywardness from Y_HWH:

> They shall not remain in the land of the Lord;
> but Ephraim shall return to Egypt,
> and in Assyria they shall eat unclean food. (Hos 9:3)
>
> *   *   *
>
> The thing itself shall be carried to Assyria
> as tribute to the great king.
> Ephraim shall be put to shame,
> and Israel shall be ashamed of his idol. (Hos 10:6)

These texts apparently anticipate a deportation to Assyria, on which see 2 Kings 17:6. Most remarkably, once in an oracle of positive anticipation, Hosea expects the return of Israelite deportees from Assyria:

> They shall come trembling like birds from Egypt
> and like doves from the land of Assyria;
> and I will return them to their homes, says the Lord. (Hos 11:11)

This cluster of texts taken altogether anticipates the way in which Jeremiah will be "a prophet to the nations" (Jer 1:10).

---

[25] See Koch, *The Prophets I*, especially 70–76.

In a variety of prophetic speeches of judgment (or judgment-speeches), Hosea assumes that Israel has violated the covenant with Yhwh *and is therefore under threat.*[26] Given the pathos of Yhwh in Hosea 2:14–15 and 11:8–9, however, even in the midst of harsh, ferocious divine judgment, the rhetoric of the prophet continues to summon Israel back into the covenant. Evidently, in the horizon of this prophet, a broken covenant did not necessarily signify termination; the prophet (and perforce Yhwh) continued to hope for a restored relationship. For the most part, the possibility of a return to Yhwh is mentioned only to declare that Israel has refused to turn.[27] Israel has been wayward (6:1) and is invited to return (14:1), but does not in fact do so (7:10). Thus, even the utilization of the motif of restoration characteristically attests to Israel's failure.

It is to be noted that in the initiative taken by Yhwh mentioned in Hosea 2:14–17 and 11:8–9, echoed in the text of 14:4, the restoration does not depend on Israel's repentance but only on Yhwh's singular initiative grounded in the reality that Yhwh's seeking love for Israel overcomes even Yhwh's legitimate wrath. At the end of the Book of Hosea, in a verse that is situated beyond judgment, it is affirmed that Israel does return, does draw close to Yhwh, and so prospers:

> They shall again live beneath my shadow,
> they shall flourish as a garden;
> they shall blossom like the vine,
> their fragrance shall be like the wine of Lebanon. (Hos 14:7)

---

[26] On "Speeches of Judgment" or "Judgment-Speech," see Claus Westermann, *Basic Forms of Prophetic Speech* (Philadelphia: Westminster, 1967).

[27] On this thesis, see A. Vanlier Hunter, *Seek the Lord! A Study of the Meaning and Function of the Exhortations in Amos, Hosea, Isaiah, Micah, and Zephaniah* (Baltimore: St. Mary's Seminary and University, 1982).

It will be evident in what follows that themes adumbrated by Hosea become the primary staples of the Jeremian tradition. Hosea, well situated in the Sinai tradition, exercises his immense poetic imagination to give the covenant depth and richness beyond the presentation of the Sinai Pericope in Exodus 19–24. In so doing, Hosea makes the covenant tradition pertinent to his own eighth-century BCE crisis in a way that is profound and even electrifying.

Third, the Book of Deuteronomy constitutes the decisive and most powerful antecedent to Jeremiah, surely providing the interpretive milieu in which the Book of Jeremiah emerged. The Book of Deuteronomy brings to precise and powerful expression the claims of covenant that are inchoate in the Sinai Pericope of Exodus 19–24. It is widely thought that the tradition of the Book of Deuteronomy emerged in the eighth–seventh centuries BCE as a powerful rearticulation of covenant traditions focused on the Torah that had been largely eclipsed in the royal ideology of Jerusalem. Given that dating for the formation of the tradition, it is not surprising that this emerging tradition imitated the treaty form of the Assyrians because this is precisely the period of Assyrian expansion that extended into Israel and placed Judah at risk. Whereas the Assyrian treaties witness the way in which the powerful Assyrian kings bound subject peoples to themselves, the Deuteronomic tradition transposed that binding maneuver whereby Israel is bound in covenant to the sovereign God YHWH. The Book of Deuteronomy, as noted by Gerhard von Rad and a number of other scholars, follows a clear structure that expresses the components of treaty making:[28]

---

[28] Gerhard von Rad, *The Problem of the Hexateuch and Other Essays* (New York: McGraw-Hill, 1966), 26–33.

- Deuteronomy 5–11 (or even 1–11) is a historical recital and review of the saving intentions of YHWH on behalf of Israel.
- Deuteronomy 12–25, the corpus of commandments, delineates the responsible obedience that is required of Israel in order to be in covenant with YHWH. It is clear that the covenantal obligations of Israel pertain to every sphere of life, for Deuteronomy intends that there be nothing in the life of Israel that falls outside the rule of YHWH.
- Deuteronomy 26:16–19, in echoing the oath of Exodus 24:3, 7, evidences the mutual oaths of fidelity that YHWH and Israel make to each other. In this act of allegiance, Israel binds itself exclusively to YHWH.
- Deuteronomy 28 (see also 27:1–26) offers a list of sanctions (blessings and curses) that constitute rewards for covenant obedience and punishment for covenant violation. It is easy to observe that in the completed text tradition the extent and force of the negative curses run well beyond the positive blessings.

We may cite four specific texts in Deuteronomy that bespeak the dynamism of this interpretive tradition:

1. The *Leitmotif* of the whole book is the *shema* of Deuteronomy 6:4–5, which is dominated by the imperative verb "listen" (i.e., obey):[29]

> Hear, O Israel: The LORD is our God, the LORD alone. You shall love the LORD your God with all your heart, and with all your soul, and with all your might. (Deut 6:4–5)

---

[29] See J. G. Janzen, "On the Most Important Word in the Shema," *VT* 37 (1987): 280–300.

The imperative "hear" immediately precludes Israel's sense of autonomy; it makes clear that the initiative for the life of Israel is held in the commanding voice of Yhwh and that Israel is on the receiving end of instruction and requirement with no option except responsive obedience. This verb, together with the entire text of the *shema*, situates Israel as a people summoned to and defined by its ready capacity to live its life on Yhwh's terms. That summons to listen recurs in Jeremiah as the defining mark of Israel. In the tradition of Jeremiah, the weight of testimony is that Israel has *not listened*, has refused to listen in its coveted autonomy, and so stands under judgment.

2. Presentation of the covenant in Deuteronomy is not engaged in nostalgia but intends that the covenant of Sinai be immediately contemporary to every new generation and every new circumstance in Israel:

> Not with our ancestors did the Lord make this covenant, but with us, who are all of us here alive today. (Deut 5:3)

Thus, the Deuteronomists, and Jeremiah after them, can insist on the conditionality of the Torah as operative and definitional in the late seventh century BCE. It is the burden of Jeremiah to articulate the ways in which even contemporary life is to be discerned and lived in such covenantal categories.

3. The dynamism reflected in Deuteronomy 5:3 is further reflected in Deuteronomy 17:18 where the king approved by Deuteronomy is instructed to read a "copy" of this Torah. Notice that the cruciality of Torah-reading is an antidote to the royal practice of accumulation and acquisitiveness that can only lead to disaster (17:16–17). More than that, the term rendered "copy" in the NRSV would seem rather to refer to a "second version"

of the Torah, a version that is removed in time and space from Sinai (see Deut 1:1–5) but immediately pertinent to a later circumstance in Israel. The notion of a "second version" indicates how the tradition of Deuteronomy is continually relevant and therefore deeply pertinent to the crisis of 587 BCE when Jeremiah worked.

4. In Deuteronomy 18:15–22, provision is made for a prophet "like Moses" to come after Moses. Taken broadly, this Torah provision anticipates an ongoing "office" in Israel whereby the radicality of covenant is perennially urged on the community. It belongs to the prophet to insist that YHWH's sovereignty pertains in concrete ways to lived public reality. Beyond that broad provision, moreover, William L. Holladay has proposed that in the final form of the tradition it is precisely Jeremiah who is the "prophet like Moses," and that the reportage on Jeremiah is deliberately shaped to make that connection.[30] To the extent that this is true, we may anticipate that Jeremiah, in his time and place, will be, according to the covenant tradition, as decisive for the destiny of Israel as was Moses in his time. Probing this daring move from Moses to Jeremiah, it is important to ponder how it is that the human speaker is entrusted with divine utterance. This human speech that became a prophetic book testified to the radical, YHWH-centered reality of all human history. Such an interpretive maneuver is bold and daring, exactly the kind to make connection between the deep crisis of Jerusalem and this remarkable tradition of Jeremiah. The tradition of Deuteronomy,

---

[30] William L. Holladay, "The Background of Jeremiah's Self-Understanding: Moses, Samuel, and Psalm 22," *JBL* 83 (1964): 153–64. See also Christopher R. Seitz, "The Prophet Moses and the Canonical Shape of Jeremiah," *ZAW* 101 (1989): 3–27.

in its anticipation of a coming prophetic voice, is exactly the interpretive environment that evoked and legitimated the tradition of
Jeremiah.

We may particularly notice three facets of this interpretive tradition of Deuteronomy that will be pertinent to our study of Jeremiah.

First, the formulation of *rewards for obedience* and *punishment
for disobedience* is exact and symmetrical, with no slippage allowed
in the relationship.[31] There is no escape from the defining reality
of YHWH's will. This symmetry is clearly expressed in the following
unit:

> See I have set before you today life and prosperity, death and adver-
> sity. If you obey the commandments of the LORD your God that I
> am commanding you today, by loving the LORD your God, walking
> in his ways, and observing his commandments, decrees, and ordi-
> nances, then you shall live and become numerous, and the LORD
> your God will bless you in the land that you are entering to possess.
> But if your heart turns away and you do not hear, but are led astray
> to bow down to other gods and serve them, I declare to you today
> that you shall perish; you shall not live long in the land that you are
> crossing the Jordan to enter and possess. I call heaven and earth to
> witness against you today that I have set before you life and death,
> blessings and curses. Choose life so that you and your descendants
> may live, loving the LORD your God, obeying him, and holding fast
> to him; for that means life to you and length of days, so that you
> may live in the land that the LORD swore to give to your ancestors,
> to Abraham, to Isaac, and to Jacob. (Deut 30:15–20)

Second, it is clear throughout the corpus of Deuteronomy that
the future of this covenantal relationship concerns the land of

---

[31] See Walter Brueggemann, "A Shape for Old Testament Theology I: Structure Legitimation," *CBQ* 47 (1985): 28–46, reprinted in *Old Testament Theology: Essays on Structure, Theme, and Text*, ed. Patrick D. Miller (Minneapolis:
Fortress, 1992), 1–21.

promise as the culmination of YHWH's goodness. This is indeed a "theology of the land."[32] In other promissory traditions, reflected in the ancestral narratives of Genesis, the land given to Israel is a free gift of the promise-making, promise-keeping God. In the tradition of Deuteronomy, however, this relationship of YHWH–Israel–land is reformulated around the decisive "if" of Torah obedience. Everything depends on obedience, and when Israel violates covenantal Torah, the land will be lost. This teaching is a remarkable one that is central to Jeremiah, who must live his vocation in the midst of Israel's land loss.

The tradition of Jeremiah and much of the Old Testament that ponders the crisis of 587 BCE understands the risk of land loss in terms according to the quite direct agency of YHWH. In this reading, YHWH will deny the land to a recalcitrant covenant partner. This "supernatural" articulation of direct divine agency, however, can be understood in a less direct way. In such a reading – which falls outside the rhetoric of Deuteronomy – there simply are, in the "material" workings of political economy, some givens, limits, and realities that must be honored for possessing the land.[33]

Third, in the late development of Deuteronomy, it is assumed that the covenant has been violated and that the land has been put

---

[32] See Patrick D. Miller, "The Gift of God: The Deuteronomic Theology of the Land," *Interpretation* 23 (1969): 451–65; and Brueggemann, *The Land*, 43–65.

[33] We might expect to find such "commonsense" observations in the sapiential traditions of the Old Testament. It is worth noting in this regard that Moshe Weinfeld has found important influences of wisdom instruction in Deuteronomy. (See his *Deuteronomy and the Deuteronomic School* [Oxford: Clarendon, 1972].) Hence, even the starchy rhetoric of Deuteronomy is not uninterested in how "the real world" works. In the "real world," land is characteristically in jeopardy when it is not inhabited and managed in a way congruent with the intrinsic character of the land.

at risk. Hans Walter Wolff has identified texts – notably Deuteronomy 4:29–31 and 30:1–10 (along with 1 Kings 8) – in which the Deuteronomic tradition summons Israel to repent and so reengages the covenant after Israel had carelessly and willfully departed it.[34] This summons to repent, perhaps addressed to the generation of Israelites after 587 BCE, forms one of the grounds for hope and future expectation. It does so, however, within the assumptions of Deuteronomy. That is, the *future (still) depends on covenantal obedience.* The good news in such texts is that YHWH "can be found" and Israel is permitted a return in obedience, albeit a return in the midst of divine judgment enacted.

The influence of Deuteronomy on the tradition of Jeremiah is immense. Indeed the "C source" *is* Deuteronomic, so that much of the prose material in Jeremiah reflects the phrasing and cadences of Deuteronomic rhetoric.[35] Beyond such obvious rhetorical kinship, however, the main point to observe is that the traditions of Jeremiah also assume a rigorous covenantal conditionality with no room for slippage. Deuteronomy imagines, as the text is given us, a scenario of covenantal disobedience together with covenantal sanctions of land loss. In Jeremiah, however, such a scenario is no longer an imagined possibility. Covenantal disobedience and the deportation from the land that is soon to follow are now a lived reality that no amount of pretense or denial can overcome.

---

[34] Hans Walter Wolff, "The Kerygma of the Deuteronomic Historical Work," in *The Vitality of Old Testament Tradition*, ed. Walter Brueggemann and Hans Walter Wolff, 2nd ed. (Atlanta: John Knox, 1982), 93–97.

[35] The relation of Jeremiah to the traditions of Deuteronomy has been much studied. Among the classic discussions are those of Henri Cazelles, "Jeremiah and Deuteronomy," in *A Prophet to the Nations: Essays in Jeremiah Studies*, ed. Leo G. Perdue and Brian W. Kovacs (Winona Lake, IN: Eisenbrauns, 1984), 89–111; and J. Philip Hyatt, "Jeremiah and Deuteronomy," in Perdue and Kovacs, *A Prophet to the Nations*, 113–27.

In sum, it is obvious that these three bodies of literature – *the Sinai Pericope, Hosea,* and *Deuteronomy* – constitute an important corpus that is antecedent to the Book of Jeremiah in many ways and on many levels.

JEREMIAH: PORTRAIT OF THE PROPHET

There is no doubt that at the core of the Book of Jeremiah is the powerful person of Jeremiah, a poet of immense imagination and a man of deep courage and faith. What we can know of Jeremiah the man, however, is deeply in dispute among current interpreters. A more traditional view, held by William L. Holladay and Jack R. Lundbom, is that the Book of Jeremiah offers reliable historical reportage on him.[36] A more radical view, advocated by Robert P. Carroll, is that we have no real access to the person of Jeremiah; rather, what we have is a constructed presentation of Jeremiah in the interest and service of a later, imposed ideology of the Deuteronomists.[37] In this view, the person of Jeremiah is simply a vehicle for an angle of vision advocated by later traditionists. The view advocated in the present study is a mediating one. I do not believe we have reportage on the person of Jeremiah; thus elsewhere I have written of a "portrait" of the prophet, a sketch offered by an intentional artist.[38] I do not believe with Carroll that this is a willfully imposed ideological

[36] For Holladay, see note 3, this chapter; for Lundbom, see Jack R. Lundbom, *Jeremiah 1–20: A New Translation with Introduction and Commentary*, AB 21 A (New York: Doubleday, 1999).

[37] In addition to Carroll's commentary cited in note 4 of this chapter, see Robert P. Carroll, *From Chaos to Covenant: Prophecy in the Book of Jeremiah* (New York: Crossroad, 1981).

[38] Walter Brueggemann, "The Book of Jeremiah: Portrait of the Prophet," in *Interpreting the Prophets*, ed. James Luther Mays and Paul J. Achtemeier (Philadelphia: Fortress, 1987), 13–29.

construct but rather the inevitable development of a portrait through the traditioning process when traditionists inescapably filter the subject through their own perceptual lens. It is possible, moreover, that the prophet himself was fully resonant with what became of the Deuteronomic tradition, so that this later "portrayal" need not be a willful imposition or an intentional ideological distortion. Thus I suggest that Jeremiah fit rather easily into the perceptual field of the covenantal theology espoused by the Deuteronomic traditionists and that he stood with and alongside a small network of persons in Jerusalem who were deeply critical of and resistant to the dominant practices of the urban establishment. The following paragraphs discuss elements that seem pertinent in a portrayal of this compelling figure.

Jeremiah, in the superscription of the book, is said to be "son of Hilkiah" (Jer 1:1). It is to be noted that in 2 Kings 22:8, the "high priest" is Hilkiah. The cruciality of this reference is that 2 Kings 22 is commonly taken to refer to the scroll of Deuteronomy. Thus the chapter stands at the center of the vigorous assertion of Deuteronomic theology, championed by King Josiah, in the midst of a royal temple venue. It is at least plausible that the Hilkiah of this narrative is the father of Jeremiah; it is certainly no more than just plausible, but the correspondence is to be noted.[39] Were the two Hilkiahs identical or even playfully entertained as identical, the connection would be an important one for linking Jeremiah to this formidable and subversive "scroll movement."

Also in Jeremiah 1:1, it is asserted that Jeremiah is "of the priests who were in Anathoth in the land of Benjamin." The mention of the village of Anathoth is important on two counts. First, this reference roots the prophet in the life and perspective of a village; that village,

---

[39] See Wilson, *Prophecy and Society in Ancient Israel*, 223.

moreover, is in the tribal territory of Benjamin, outside of Jerusalem and outside of Judah, and so outside the immediate sphere of royal temple influence. The importance of village rootage is that in the royal economy of the Jerusalem establishment, villages populated by peasants served basically to provide tax money to support the central establishment and produce agricultural goods to enhance the royal economy. On both counts, it is plausible, even likely, that the village perspective is deeply resentful of affluent urban life. Moreover, it is evident in the narrative of Jeremiah 32:1–15 that a traditional, tribal understanding of land as family inheritance is operative in the book – a notion of land that surely resisted the commoditization of land under royal decree.[40] We may thus expect that Jeremiah was nurtured in a perspective that was, from the ground up, highly suspicious of the political, economic, and theological pretensions of the urban establishment.

But, second and more important, the reference to "Anathoth" in Jeremiah 1:1 draws us back into the memory and tradition of Israel to the priest Abiathar. Abiathar, son of a priestly family, had signed on with David at a risky moment in his life and at a critical moment in the life of David (1 Sam 22:11–23). Abiathar faithfully served David as priest alongside Zadok (2 Sam 15:24–29). At the death of David, however, Abiathar – as a formidable figure in the royal court – sided with Adonijah in the struggle for royal succession (1 Kings 1:7–8). Abiathar had backed the loser; consequently, the winner, Solomon, in retaliation against his opponents, exiled Abiathar to his village of Anathoth:

> The king said to the priest Abiathar, "Go to Anathoth, to your estate; for you deserve death. But I will not at this time put you to death,

---

[40] See D. N. Premnath, *Eighth Century Prophets: A Social Analysis* (St. Louis, MO: Chalice, 2003).

because you carried the ark of the LORD God before my father David, and because you shared in all the hardships my father endured." (1 Kings 2:26)

Solomon had killed all of the other opponents but apparently was reluctant to kill a priest. It is important to notice that 1 Kings 2:27 alludes to an even older prophetic oracle in 1 Samuel 2:33. That text alludes to Abiathar of the house of Eli, who will "weep his eyes out":

> The only one of you whom I shall not cut off from my altar shall be spared to weep out his eyes and grieve his heart; all the members of your household shall die by the sword. (1 Sam 2:33)

These references place Abiathar – and presumably many generations of his family after him – in the village of Anathoth. It is most probable, then, that the connection of Jeremiah to "the priests of Anathoth" intends to connect Jeremiah directly to Abiathar. The importance of this is that this family of priests, sustained over long generations, had long been opposed to the ostentatious self-indulgence of the Davidic house in its trajectory of economic–military autonomy on which Solomon had set it. This means that Jeremiah was a product and representative of a theology grounded in hostility to the Davidic establishment that is both very old and very deep.

Jeremiah is presented as a man who not only carried on a prophetic polemic against the Jerusalem establishment (as in Jer 22:13–19, 28–30) but became a confidant of King Zedekiah (21:1–7; 37:3–10; 38:14–28; 39:11–14). We do not know how a village outsider might have gained access to the king, who placed some confidence in him. The initiatives from the side of King Zedekiah were no doubt acts of acute desperation when all else had failed. In any case, Jeremiah is presented as a force to be reckoned with in the public life of Jerusalem, no doubt because there were no alternatives, and perhaps because his utterances, unpopular as they were, became increasingly compelling in a time of deep crisis.

Two other features about Jeremiah's public life are worth noting. First, Jeremiah is clearly connected with the important and influential *scribes*, learned men who could write and who produced scrolls that endured as lasting testimony to the legacy of prophetic utterance. In particular, Jeremiah is connected with Baruch, son of Neriah, a scribe who produced the scroll that eventually became the Book of Jeremiah (36:4).[41] Baruch was intimately connected with Jeremiah and suffered with Jeremiah for their daring testimony (Jer 43:1–7). A second son of Neriah, Seraiah, is also in the service of Jeremiah and is commissioned to deliver a daring, subversive oracular word against Babylon (Jer 51:59–64). These particular connections help to link Jeremiah to what must have been an important political force in Jerusalem. Beyond that, the Jeremiah–Baruch connection surely embodies and reflects the move in emerging Judaism from *prophetic utterance* to *scribal scroll*. That connection goes far in suggesting how the utterance of the man became a prophetic book, a book preserved by scribes to bear abiding testimony against the self-destructive policies of the royal temple urban elites.

Alongside a scribal connection, secondly, it is to be noted that Jeremiah – for all his subversive utterances – benefits from the quiet but firm support of the family of Shaphan. Shaphan was apparently a powerful presence in the small political economy of Jerusalem, and his family keeps showing up at crucial places in the career of Jeremiah, in protective support for the prophet:

> But the hand of Ahikam son of Shaphan was with Jeremiah so that he was not given over into the hands of the people to be put to death. (Jer 26:24)

---

[41] See James Muilenburg, "Baruch the Scribe," in Perdue and Kovacs, *A Prophet to the Nations*, 229–45.

So Nebuzaradan the captain of the guard, Nebushazban the Rabsaris, Nergal-sharezer the Rabmag, and all the chief officers of the king of Babylon sent and took Jeremiah from the court of the guard. They entrusted him to Gedaliah son of Ahikam son of Shaphan to be brought home. So he stayed with his own people. (Jer 39:13–14; see 40:5)[42]

The fact that Jeremiah had such powerful political allies and protectors suggests that he was not a lone voice in Jerusalem. Rather, he represented a point of view that had some important adherents in Jerusalem who supported Jeremiah as a voice for their perspective. From the side of Shaphan, support for the prophet, and consequently opposition to the king, was a dangerous and daring position, one taken at great risk. Thus, the support of Jeremiah in such risk was surely understood to be a life-or-death matter, not only a deep personal risk for the prophet but one concerning make-or-break public policies.

These elements of personal history – *rooted in Abiathar, supported in the scribal community*, and *protected by Shaphan* – altogether suggest that Jeremiah is located in a subversive body of opinion in Jerusalem that was opposed to royal policy and that supported Jeremiah as the point person for more widely but dangerously held views. Certainly Jeremiah – and apparently his entire subcommunity – concluded that the royal temple establishment, in its alienation from older covenant traditions, was practicing policies of death and destruction.

Given such a political location, we may identify three facets of what seemed to be the thrust of the utterances of Jeremiah. First, rooted in the Sinai tradition (which as we have seen also pertains to Hosea and Deuteronomy), the prophet judged that covenantal

---

[42] It is important to note that in these traditions there is a second Shaphan, surely not to be confused with the head of the powerful family related to Jeremiah.

commands (especially the First Commandment, on exclusive loyalty) had been violated so that covenantal curses were operative against Jerusalem. The combination of *covenantal commands* and *covenantal curses* as sanctions eventuated in a judgment-speech consisting of *indictment and sentence.*[43] The judgment-speech became the stock-in-trade pattern of utterance in the pre-exilic prophets, all of whom in various ways observed that covenantal violation would inescapably lead to huge trouble, inflicted according to the will of YHWH. That same basic rhetorical pattern dominates the utterances of Jeremiah. He lived close to the crisis point that emerged in 587 BCE concerning the destruction of Jerusalem; his rhetoric appropriately is one of graphic intensity and emotional extremity.

Second, the primary pattern of *indictment and sentence,* a rather symmetrical conventional model, is filtered through Jeremiah's acute personal experience of God. In addition to the direct encounter of the "call narrative" of Jeremiah 1:4–10, the "Lamentations of Jeremiah" bespeak a man who is intensely engaged with and acutely confronted by the reality of God.[44] These poems evidence an acute wrestling with God in which Jeremiah is summoned and dispatched by YHWH with a vocation that is so costly as to be unbearable. YHWH promises to be steadfastly supportive of Jeremiah but at the same time is presented as hard-nosed and unyielding, holding

[43] Westermann, *Basic Forms of Prophetic Speech,* provides the best survey of the material and the function of the form.

[44] The texts include Jeremiah 11:18–12:6; 15:10–21; 17:14–18; 18:18–23; and 20:7–13. See the discussions in Kathleen M. O'Connor, *The Confessions of Jeremiah: Their Interpretation and Their Role in Chapters 1–25,* SBLDS 94 (Atlanta: Scholars Press, 1987); A. R. Diamond, *The Confessions of Jeremiah in Context: Scenes of Prophetic Drama,* JSOTSup 47 (Sheffield: Sheffield Academic Press, 1987); and Mark S. Smith, *The Laments of Jeremiah and Their Contexts: A Literary and Redactional Study of Jeremiah 11–20,* SBLMS 42 (Atlanta: Scholars Press, 1990).

Jeremiah to his vocation. Although the lamentations present deep problems for interpretation, there is little doubt that they evidence a theological confrontation of immense depth that scarred and engaged the prophetic personality and so gave profound force to his utterance – an utterance the prophet was compelled to offer against his own will. Clearly, Jeremiah is more than a social critic or a traditionalist, though he is both of these. Beyond that, he is a man of deep spiritual turmoil to whom was given a radically alternative sense of historical reality.

Third, as a result of the tradition of prophetic *judgment-speeches* combined with an acute *spiritual rawness* and *directness*, the utterance of Jeremiah concerning public policy in Jerusalem is articulated with wondrous and imaginative poetic freedom and force. While the message of Jeremiah is relentless in its constancy, it continues to interest and empower us because poetic freedom – that is, prophetic imagination – uses rich variety and variation amid the constancy of the message.[45] Thus, the deathliness under which Jerusalem lives is, for example, variously exposed as foreign invasion at the behest of YHWH (4:14–17), marital fickleness that can only end in rejection and divorce (3:1–6), and terminal illness for which there is no healing (8:18–9:3). The hearer of this strange poetry must pay attention to the detail and the nuance as the poet labors imaginatively to penetrate the recalcitrant hard-heartedness of the power elites of Jerusalem.

The outcome of this consideration of the person of Jeremiah is that he is a singular artistic voice in Jerusalem with a countermessage. That countermessage, however, is not a private one; rather, it is

---

[45] Such a performance of alternative reality in the text of Jeremiah is the quintessential expression of "prophetic imagination" to which I have given exposition in *The Prophetic Imagination*, 2nd ed. (Minneapolis: Fortress, 2001).

championed at some risk by a powerful urban alliance in Jerusalem. Thus the prophet Jeremiah moves back and forth between the dangerous political venue of the city and the deep rootage of the village, and in that movement he is given words that tell the truth about the death of Jerusalem and the lean prospects for life. This the prophet sees clearly and says unmistakably that the city is in a life-or-death moment.

JUDGMENT AND HOPE, POETRY AND PROSE

The poetry of Jeremiah is poignant and compelling. It is, however, sometimes complex and unclear. There stands alongside the poetry, however, a body of prose material that at times parallels, at times supplants, and at times comments on the poetry. While this prose material is variously judged to be from the prophet (by Holladay and Lundbom) or from the Deuteronomist (by Carroll), either way it functions as a second wave of testimony concerning YHWH's sovereignty over the crisis facing Jerusalem. As might be expected, the prose material is more didactic and functions in a more or less thematizing way. In that regard, it is unlike the poetry, for poetry, in its very articulation, resists any thematization that runs in the direction of reductionism or explanation.

The thematization of the prose material clusters around the themes of *judgment* (with a summons to repent) and *hope*. This twofold theme governs the final form of the Book of Jeremiah as it interprets and comments on the crisis of 587 BCE. The theme of judgment concerns the destruction of Jerusalem at the hands of the Babylonians because it has been a fickle partner to YHWH. The theme of hope is a pondering of the Book of Jeremiah after the judgment to see what future, if any, can still be entertained by this city under judgment.

Both themes, judgment and hope, are profoundly YHWH-centered, for it is YHWH who will terminate Jerusalem and it is YHWH who will give a future to the city. The theme of judgment is mediated and enacted through historical agency, notably the Babylonians. But the theme of hope, "the conviction of things not seen" (Heb 11:1), is an act of buoyant imagination *beyond* historical evidence. It is a work of imagination that relies exclusively on confidence in YHWH's enduring purpose.

This twofold theme is very old in the covenantal traditions of Israel in which Jeremiah is grounded. We have seen that "sanctions" in the Sinai Pericope are at best inchoate (Exod 23:20–33). In later, more developed covenantal traditions, these themes are highly visible. Thus, in the long poem of Hosea 2, that prophetic tradition, through the imagery of divorce and remarriage, traces devastating judgment upon Israel (vv. 2–13) and hope (vv. 14–23) that is, astonishingly, wrought through YHWH's yearning for a new relationship. In Hosea, the prospect of hope is grounded in a new, generous initiative on YHWH's part, an initiation that is rooted in YHWH's own pathos-filled love.[46]

The matter is very different in the traditions of Deuteronomy because Deuteronomy, in its symmetrical pattern, declared that blessings and curses are meted out in strict response to obedience or disobedience (Deut 11:22–28; 30:15–20). Within that framework, the enactment of a covenantal curse in response to disobedience forecloses any future; blessings are given only to the obedient (Deut 28:1–14). Deuteronomy is clear in an uncompromising way

---

[46] On divine pathos, see Abraham J. Heschel, *The Prophets* (New York: Harper and Row, 1962); H. Wheeler Robinson, *The Cross in the Old Testament* (Philadelphia: Westminster, 1955); and Kazo Kitamori, *Theology of the Pain of God* (Richmond, VA: John Knox, 1965).

regarding what I have elsewhere called "structure legitimization."[47] It is clear, however, that such a symmetrical pattern, taken by itself, is not sustainable because it offers no prospect for those already under judgment. So, in the more developed Deuteronomic tradition, there is the prospect of repentance that posits a new grant of YHWH's generosity – but, importantly, only on condition of a return to obedience (see Deut 4:29–31; 30:1–10; 1 Kings 8:33–53). Even in the "starchiness" of Deuteronomy, a way to the future is opened; it is, however, not an easy way. It depends completely on reembracing the covenant and resolving to obey the commands that Deuteronomy had articulated initially. Thus, even in this reach toward the future, Deuteronomy remains largely within a framework of obedience as a (pre)condition.

With the background of Sinai and its inchoate articulation of the covenant plus the traditions of Hosea and Deuteronomy, the prose of the Book of Jeremiah, situated in the most acute crisis of ancient Israel, thematizes the poetry of the prophet around judgment and hope. This is accomplished in its most vigorous articulation around the six verbs that culminate in the prophetic call narrative in Jeremiah 1:10:

> See, today I appoint you over
> nations and over kingdoms,
> to pluck up and to pull down,
> to destroy and to overthrow,
> to build and to plant. (Jer 1:10)

The four negative verbs – pluck up, tear down, destroy, and overthrow – refer in context to the destruction of Jerusalem, the razing of the temple and the city, and the termination of the Davidic

---

[47] See note 31, this chapter.

house. The two positive verbs – plant and build – refer to the restoration of the city (and the temple and perhaps the monarchy) after the destruction. It is clear in 1:4–10 that the prophet, according to this rendering, is not only to *report* on these two actions but is to *effect* these actions by performed utterance. Jeremiah, in prophetic speech, is to *do* what he is to *say*. It is evident that the multiple uses of this set of verbs (see 12:14–17; 18:1–11; 24:4–7; 31:27–30; 45:4) are used in a variety of ways, no doubt in different circumstances to accent different points in the framework of judgment and hope. It is to be observed, moreover, that all of these usages occur in prose passages, a fact that suggests an imposed thematization on the more indeterminate poetic utterance of the prophet. It is clear in my judgment, nonetheless, that this is not an alien imposition on the poetry but that it in fact resonates closely with the general perspective offered in the poetic utterance. The thematization resonates with poetic utterance because at the core of the prophetic claim is the conviction that YHWH will indeed judge a recalcitrant city, dynasty, and people. But an equally compelling conviction is at the same core: that YHWH does not – cannot and will not – quit at that nadir point, precisely because YHWH's most elemental passion is for this people.[48] Thus, the move beyond radical judgment is rooted, according to prophetic imagination, in YHWH's own elemental resolve.

Given the rawness of prophetic utterance and given the more symmetrical thematization of this raw prophetic utterance in prose, we may return to the source analysis of Duhn and Mowinckel noted earlier that identified sources A, B, and C, respectively – "namely," Jeremiah, Baruch, and the Deuteronomist. This way of thinking

---

[48] See Walter Zimmerli, *I Am Yahweh* (Atlanta: John Knox, 1982), 11–33.

served nineteenth-century methods about literary clumsiness and complexity. Without denying that multivoiced complexity, we may nevertheless notice how the several voices converge in their primal claims. The "Baruch connection" in the Book of Jeremiah no doubt refers to the dimension of scribal interest in bringing the book to its final form, so that during exile and after exile the scribes became the shapers of Judaism and the preservers of extant prophetic utterance.[49] Such scribes, however, did not arise de novo. In important ways, they are the true heirs of Deuteronomic theology, which was already a "scroll movement" of irresistible force that offered its "scroll vision" as an alternative to the self-destructive policies of the dominant (royal) urban elites. In this light, what Duhm and Mowinckel called the "B" and "C" sources nicely converge. Behind that, however, we may suggest that Jeremiah was not an isolated individual figure but that he was located – politically and theologically – in the community of opposition that featured both Deuteronomic interests (Shaphan?) and scribal interests (Baruch). Thus, the convergence of poetry, political criticism, and scribal work is theologically rooted in political opposition to dynasty and temple. The core conviction of this convergence is that submission to Babylonian power is the way to survival, a submission that is in fact the will of Yhwh. That submission envisioned the loss of political independence and the forfeiture of the primal symbols of Judaism, both theological and liturgical. This scroll movement, however, did not flinch from such submission and forfeiture because it believed that the scrolls it had generated and preserved (see 2 Kings 22; Jer 36) constituted an adequate resource that would fund the enterprise of Judaism – if it were to succeed at all – in terms of Torah

---

[49] See Philip R. Davies, *Scribes and Schools: The Canonization of the Hebrew Scriptures*, LAI (Louisville, KY: Westminster John Knox, 1998).

visions that were rooted in Moses. Thus the passionate conviction of this convergence of opposition is nicely articulated: "Better
Babylonian than destroyed," or "Better red than dead." That acute
perspective, however, is grounded not in pragmatism but in a deep
theological conviction that Yhwh's will, in the end, will prevail.
Although the God who plucks up and tears down enacts the loss
of city, temple, and dynasty, that same God is capable of planting
and building anew.

This last point – that God can plant and build – causes us finally
to focus on *the theme of hope* in the Book of Jeremiah. That theme
is not as deeply developed as the theme of judgment. It is, however, decisively voiced in the final form of the text. Hope is the
overriding theme of chapters 30–33; moreover, the Oracles Against
the Nations in chapters 46–51 envisioned the defeat of Israel's enemies to the great benefit of Israel. What is to be noted about this
remarkable voice of hope is that it does not grow "naturally" out
of the covenantal constraints of Deuteronomy, for in that tradition the future depends on repentance. The radical articulation
of hope in the Book of Jeremiah concerns Yhwh's singular intention, which does not depend on Israel's repentance. We conclude
that such hope is a genuine *novum* in the Book of Jeremiah.[50]
That hope cannot be understood in terms of antecedent traditions but is in fact a great theological leap beyond Deuteronomic
symmetry. Although the leap may be informed by geopolitical reality (the Persian defeat of Babylon), in truth the leap of hope is a

---

[50] See Walter Brueggemann, "The Travail of Pardon: Reflections on *slḥ*," in *A God
So Near: Essays on Old Testament Theology in Honor of Patrick D. Miller*, ed.
Brent A. Strawn and Nancy R. Bowen (Winona Lake, IN: Eisenbrauns, 2003),
283–97. See also Thomas M. Raitt, *A Theology of Exile: Judgment/Deliverance
in Jeremiah and Ezekiel* (Philadelphia: Fortress, 1977), which argues similarly
for Jeremiah and also for Ezekiel.

theological one rooted in the fresh initiative of YHWH in the life of Israel and in a fresh voicing of YHWH's initiative through prophetic imagination.

CONCLUSION

In the end, then, the Book of Jeremiah is a remarkable interpretive struggle concerning *the continuity* of Israel's life with YHWH that is rooted in YHWH's commitment and concerns *the discontinuity* in Israel's life with YHWH that is caused by severe judgment. The resolution of the matter of continuity and discontinuity is not an easy one, and different texts – in different circumstances and from different perspectives – offer different nuances. Christian interpretative practice has tended to side – often glibly – with continuity. But the situation according to the tradition of Jeremiah is not so obvious. It is not obvious because of the elusive quality of YHWH's engagement in the life of the world. It is not so obvious, furthermore, because of the inscrutability of the historical process. Every concentration of power and meaning (such as nation-state or church) prefers to think that it is guaranteed to go on "forever." In our time, however, we have watched the termination of the Soviet Union and of the apartheid regime in South Africa, both of which seemed destined to continue in perpetuity. The issue is therefore as contemporary in our time as it was in old Jerusalem. So, it is important to remember, in observing negotiations on this question in the text, that the makers of the texts and the formers of the Book of Jeremiah themselves did not know what God would do or what the destiny of Jerusalem would be. It is for this reason that the text is able to say:

> For thus says the LORD: The whole land shall be a desolation; yet I will not make a full end. (Jer 4:27)

Peter R. Ackroyd has explored one suggestive way in which continuity is maintained in the tradition by attention to the "temple vessels" that were deported and lost but subsequently restored.[51] Such concrete aspects of loss and recovery are crucial "visible signs," but they speak at best darkly about the "invisible reality" that remains hidden even amid the signs. It is in this way that the Book of Jeremiah – a complex convergence of prophetic utterance, political realism, and scribal attentiveness – ponders the crisis of 587 BCE. It invites the reading community up to, into, and back out of the abyss, at every point testifying to the one who is the Lord of the abyss.[52]

---

[51] Peter R. Ackroyd, "The Temple Vessels: A Continuity Theme," in his *Studies in the Religious Tradition of the Old Testament* (London: SCM, 1987), 46–60.

[52] See Walter Brueggemann, "Meditation upon the Abyss: The Book of Jeremiah," *WW* 22 (2002): 340–50.

CHAPTER 2

The Theology of the Book of Jeremiah

GOD AS SOVEREIGN

The Book of Jeremiah is preoccupied with a profound, long-term historical crisis that concerns both Judah (Jerusalem) and the international geopolitical milieu of Judah. That historical crisis, however, is outlined in the Book of Jeremiah with definitive reference to the will, purpose, action, and character of Yhwh, the God of Israel. Indeed, the effect of prophetic rhetoric in the prophets in general and in Jeremiah in particular is to link in decisive ways the *rule of* Yhwh and the *lived reality of history*. This connection is accomplished precisely through imaginative rhetoric that yields what Klaus Koch has termed "meta-history"; that is, public history understood and presented as an arena of God's purpose and activity.[1] A theological exposition of the Book of Jeremiah therefore must begin with the character and action of Yhwh outlined in prophetic rhetoric.

It is clear in all parts of the Book of Jeremiah that Yhwh, the God of the long-established covenant tradition, is now seen to be the decisive agent in the Jerusalem of the seventh through sixth

---

[1] See Klaus Koch, *The Prophets I: The Assyrian Period* (Philadelphia: Fortress, 1982), 70–76 and passim.

centuries BCE in a way that the dominant opinion in Jerusalem could scarcely countenance. Of the much rich material on this subject, we may consider the following texts.

Near the end of the Book of Jeremiah, when YHWH is juxtaposed with the overstated illicit power of Babylon (and the Babylonian gods), YHWH's self-declaration offers a ringing, triumphal affirmation of YHWH as incomparable in power and legitimacy:

> For *who* is like me? *Who* can summon me? *Who* is the shepherd who can stand before me? Therefore hear the plan that the LORD has made against Babylon, and the purposes that he has formed against the land of the Chaldeans. (Jer 50:44b–45a)

This defiant self-announcement is voiced in three rhetorical questions, "Who . . . Who . . . Who?" The answer to all three questions is, of course, "No one." *No one* is like YHWH and *no one* can summon YHWH. *No one* can stand before YHWH. Therefore, even mighty, pretentious Babylon must heed the "plan" and "purpose" of YHWH, which is precisely to dismantle the mighty power of Babylon. The reason Babylon must be terminated is because it has "arrogantly defied" the rule of YHWH (Jer 50:29), and this defiance will not go unchecked. This "formula of incomparability" is a proper starting point from which to discern the claim of YHWH that dominates the rhetoric and the faith of the Book of Jeremiah.[2] YHWH is without rival or competitor in power, for YHWH's power is massive and unlimited. YHWH's power, moreover, has a kind of legitimacy that no rival power can claim, precisely because this is the true God to whom all are eventually accountable.

---

[2] On the formula, see Walter Brueggemann, *Theology of the Old Testament: Testimony, Dispute, Advocacy* (Minneapolis: Fortress, 1997), 139–44; and the classic study of C. J. Labuschagne, *The Incomparability of Yahweh in the Old Testament* (Leiden: Brill, 1966).

When the Book of Jeremiah ends, the unrivaled sovereignty of YHWH concerns the claim that even the nations that do not confess YHWH are finally accountable to YHWH's hidden yet effective purpose. That purpose is characteristically expressed in the verb "stir up" (*'wr*), which makes a claim that is quite specific but, at the same time, remarkably elusive:

> For I am going to *stir up* [*mē'îr*] and bring against Babylon a company of great nations from the land of the north; and they shall array themselves against her; from there she shall be taken. Their arrows are like the arrows of a skilled warrior who does not return empty-handed. (Jer 50:9)

> Thus says the LORD:

> I am going to *stir up* [*mē'îr*] a destructive wind against Babylon and against the inhabitants of Lebqamai. (Jer 51:1)

> The LORD has *stirred up* [*hē'îr*] the spirit of the kings of the Medes, because his purpose concerning Babylon is to destroy it, for that is the vengeance of the LORD, vengeance for his temple. (Jer 51:11 b)

This is a characteristic way in which it is asserted that YHWH's governance is comprehensive, massive, and irresistible. The Book of Jeremiah culminates in a late passage with a great international (cosmic) vision of the way in which all parties must submit, either in willing obedience or in disastrous judgment (chapter 25).

The formula of incomparability, in large scope, pertains to the nations of the world. But before that large vista is considered, the same formula is voiced concerning Judah's recalcitrance and the truth that, even in Jerusalem, all must come to terms with this unrivaled God. The poetic passage in Jeremiah 10:1–17 gathers the key aspects of this claim of incomparability together. On the one hand, the poem critiques the empty, pretentious claims of the idols, the other gods toward whom Jerusalem is tempted.

The characteristic rhetoric of the attack on the idols is a mock-ing, sarcastic dismissal of both the other gods and the makers and adherents of those gods, who imagine that humanly constructed objects of worship can have any power or make any difference. Amid the threefold dismissal of nongods (10:2–5, 8–9, 14–15), YHWH is praised and affirmed as the creator God who can generate and sustain life and who will be feared. The initial doxological affirma-tion begins with the formula of incomparability in verse 6 that is answered with the second such formula in verse 7:

> There is none like you, O LORD;
> you are great, and your name is great in might.
> Who would not fear you, O King of the nations?
> For that is your due;
> among all the wise ones of the nations
> and in all their kingdoms
> there is no one like you. (Jer 10:6–7)

The second assertion concerning YHWH becomes more specific about YHWH's power as creator:

> It is he who made the earth by his power,
> who established the world by his wisdom,
> and by his understanding stretched out the heavens.
> When he utters his voice, there is a tumult of waters in the heavens,
> and he makes the mist rise from the ends of the earth.
> He makes lightnings for the rain,
> and he brings out the wind from his storehouses. (Jer 10:12–13)[3]

This is the God who made, who established, who stretched out all creation. The threefold assertion of verse 12 is detailed in verse 13

---

[3] In the Hebrew text, these verses begin with a participle and without any specified subject. The matter is clarified in the LXX by explicit reference to God.

as the God who supervises all aspects of creation: waters, mist, lightning, wind (see Job 38–41; Pss 147:15–18; 148:5–16). In Jeremiah 10:16, a different sort of formula of incomparability is articulated concerning the God who, unlike the pitiful idols, "formed all things":

> Not like these is the LORD,
> the portion of Jacob,
> for he is the one who formed all things. (Jer 10:16a)

But then, in a remarkable maneuver, verse 16b concludes the rhetorical unit with a characteristic move from the large sphere of creation, with an accent on *divine power*, to the specificity of Israel, with an accent on *divine fidelity*:

> And Israel is the tribe of his inheritance;
> the LORD of hosts is his name. (Jer 10:16b)

The God of all creation is the God who has taken Israel as a singularly cherished possession. By the end of the poem, it is clear that the claims of creation are all mobilized toward Israel. On the one hand, such a rhetorical maneuver offers immense assurance to Israel as the people of YHWH. On the other hand, as all creation and all nations must "fear" YHWH, so Israel is bound to YHWH in obedience. The dramatic statement of verse 16, "The LORD of Hosts is his name," is a characteristic doxological formula bespeaking YHWH's own unparalleled power as the one who is LORD of creation and who governs the historical process (see Amos 4:13; 5:8; 9:6).

This poem in Jeremiah 10:1–16 is located in the Book of Jeremiah at the conclusion of chapters 8–9, a subunit that is concerned with Israel's recalcitrance and waywardness. This passage thus functions to assert Israel's precarious position vis-à-vis this God who would cherish this peculiar people.

It is important to notice that the doxology to the creator in Jeremiah 10:12–13 that eventually pertains to Israel in verse 16 is reiterated in 51:15–16, together with a mocking of the gods in 51:17–18. In this belated, second context, the massive power of YHWH is displayed vis-à-vis the recalcitrant nations (Babylon), just as it is displayed in chapter 10 vis-à-vis Israel. This lively doxology thus functions to assert divine sovereignty equally over Israel and over the nations, or, as we might say, equally in the arena of redemption as in the arena of creation.

The remarkable characterization of YHWH as the sovereign God, marked by a formula of incomparability concerning both power and fidelity, is sounded somewhat differently in 23:23–24, a passage that goes on to speak of true and false prophets. In the first two verses of that textual unit, however, important claims are made for YHWH:

> Am I a God nearby, says the LORD, and not a God far off? Who can hide in secret places so that I cannot see them? says the LORD. Do I not fill heaven and earth? says the LORD. (Jer 23:23–24)

Again, we are confronted with rhetorical questions with clearly implied answers. It was everywhere known in Jerusalem that YHWH was "a God nearby" (see Deut 4:7). Indeed, it is a primary claim of temple theology in Jerusalem that YHWH is present in the temple (Ps 46:1). That claim made it possible to conclude that YHWH would be the protector, patron, and guarantor of the city. Indeed, such a claim invited presumption upon YHWH, as though Jerusalem had been given a blank check of support by YHWH.

The accent in the text is thus on the quality of YHWH's life, which is marked not by nearness but by remoteness, a special image that conveys the transcendence of YHWH, who will *not* be domesticated into any of Jerusalem's pet projects. The three rhetorical questions here make the proper answer plain:

> *Yes*, this is a God far off;
> *No*, no one can hide from Yhwh;
> *Yes*, Yhwh fills heaven and earth.

The God of this text is not a warm, fuzzy God, or in Abraham J. Heschel's words, this God is no "nice uncle." Rather, this is a God who *stands over* and *apart from*, who has a distinct purpose on the earth, and who will have no one as a permanent ally. In context, this characterization of Yhwh amounts to a refutation of the easy assurances of prophets within the Jerusalem ideology who uncritically counted on the patronage of Yhwh for the sake of the urban royal temple establishment (see Jer 7:4).

It is easy to see, in the belated, desperate petition of King Zedekiah to the prophet, how the establishment was tempted to presume upon Yhwh (21:1–12). The king is at his wits' end and is without resources. As a desperate fallback position, Zedekiah asks that the prophet seek divine guidance in the face of the Babylonian threat:

> Please inquire of the Lord on our behalf, for King Nebuchadrezzar of Babylon is making war against us; perhaps the Lord will perform a wonderful deed for us, as he has often done, and will make him withdraw from us. (Jer 21:2)

The king apparently reasons that when Yhwh sees the jeopardy in which beloved Jerusalem stands, Yhwh may act decisively on behalf of the city. It is clear that Zedekiah knew the theological tradition of Israel well. He knew that Yhwh's reputation in Israel was through an accumulation of "wonderful deeds" that constituted the core of Israel's faith recital. As far back as the Exodus, Yhwh has disclosed power and fidelity toward Israel by enacting transformative deeds of rescue and liberation that are completely inexplicable, giving

Yhwh's people life even when they are pushed beyond their own resources or their capacity to cope. Zedekiah was surely a part of the community that sang doxologies summarizing the normative faith of Israel, such as the following:

> One generation shall laud your works to another,
> and shall declare your mighty acts.
> On the glorious splendor of your majesty,
> and on your wondrous works, I will meditate.
> The might of your awesome deeds shall be proclaimed,
> and I will declare your greatness.
> They shall celebrate the fame of your abundant goodness,
> and shall sing aloud of your righteousness. (Ps 145:4–7)

In this regard, the king and the prophet whom he addresses share a common faith. Both know Yhwh as the one who does impossible miracles. In the prophetic horizon, however, the huge miscalculation of the king is that he anticipates that Yhwh is on call to enact yet another miracle. The king cannot compute the reality that Yhwh is so alienated by disobedient Jerusalem that no such miracle is about to happen. In short, the king *presumes* for himself (and presumes too much) on the basis of a rich theological inheritance.

The prophetic response (Jer 21:3–7) to the royal request in verses 3–7 is a complete contradiction of royal expectation. The prophet agrees that this is a God who does wonders. But then the prophet characterizes the divine impossibility that is about to happen. This miracle is that Yhwh will act *against* Jerusalem. As William L. Moran has noted, the language of verse 5 is the rhetoric of the Exodus; only now the rhetoric that heretofore has been positive, even salvific for Israel, is turned against Jerusalem.[4]

---

[4] See William L. Moran, "The End of the Unholy War and the Anti-Exodus," *Biblica* 44 (1963): 333–42.

The God who does wonders is the God who will enact a disaster on
Yhwh's own people. Quite clearly, the God of this prophetic tradition, unlike the idols who can be "nailed down as patrons," is a
free God who is not bound to Israel in any ultimate way. This God
can act freely, even devastatingly, to exhibit divine freedom and
sovereignty.

So it is that the sovereign freedom of Yhwh, articulated as both
power and fidelity, pertains to both Israel and the nations. Yhwh's
rule over the nations pertains generically to all nations (see Jer 46–
51). That said, it is quite clear that the specific preoccupation of the
Book of Jeremiah is the *rule of Babylon under Nebuchadnezzar in
the sixth century* BCE. As John Hill has shown, Yhwh's relationship to Babylon is complex.[5] We have seen that, at the end of the
book, Yhwh is against Babylon and will destroy it by "stirring up"
a new adversary, surely Cyrus the Persian. The strategy of the Book
of Jeremiah, however, depends on the claim that Yhwh is initially
allied with Babylon and recruits Babylon as a tool for the accom-
plishment of a divine purpose. That divine purpose is the severe
punishment of Jerusalem. It is particularly evident in the divine
oracle of Jeremiah 27:4–7b. Yhwh's announcement there, "It is I,"
is grounds for claiming all of creation as the venue for Yhwh's rule,
including, of course, Babylon:

> *It is I* who by my great power and my outstretched arm have made
> the earth, with the people and animals that are on the earth, and I
> give it to whomever I please. (Jer 27:5)

The scope of divine sovereignty is evident in the formula, "I give
it [i.e., power] to whomever I please" (see Dan 4:25, 32). In this

---

[5] John Hill, *Friend or Foe? The Figure of Babylon in the Book of Jeremiah*, BIS 40
(Leiden: Brill, 1999).

particular sixth-century context, it "pleases" Yhwh to give power to Babylon. In the context of Jerusalem, this is an extraordinary display of divine freedom, for anyone in Jerusalem would expect Yhwh's pleasure to involve the decisive protection of Jerusalem from Babylon. Yhwh, however, is free, and Yhwh will claim even Nebuchadnezzar as "my servant":

> Now I have given all these lands into the hand of King Nebuchadnezzar of Babylon, my servant, and I have given him even the wild animals of the field to serve him. (Jer 27:6)

In verse 5, all animals are subject to Yhwh; in verse 6, all wild animals are subject to Nebuchadnezzar, "my servant" (see 25:9). The durability of divine freedom, however, is made clear with the "until" of 27:7b, which severely limits Nebuchadnezzar's scope of activity, and, in the end, reduces "my servant" to wholesale slavery. Thus, even in recruiting and displaying Nebuchadnezzar as "my servant," Yhwh retains complete freedom and initiative over the public process of history. Nebuchadnezzar can be cast off by divine purpose as readily as he can be utilized. As a case study in international politics, it is clear in this horizon that Nebuchadnezzar is kept completely off-balance by the intensity of divine power and freedom – power and freedom that enable a genuine *newness* that is truly imaginable in the public process.

As Yhwh's remarkable *goodness* is made plain with reference to the nations, that same elusive divinity is made manifest regarding the particularity of Israel and Jerusalem. To that end, we may cite three texts.

In the first text, Jeremiah 15:6–9, the prophet delivers a harsh judgment on Jerusalem because "you have rejected me." As a result of that rejection of a summons to obedience, Yhwh details an extended speech of judgment against the city. The hand that had stretched out the heavens is now stretched out "against you" (v. 8). Yʜwʜ has dispatched a destroyer (probably Babylon) that has brought anguish, terror, shame, disgrace, and evidently the sword with much death in its wake. Yʜwʜ will not be "rejected" with impunity. What is most interesting in this text is verse 5:

> Who will have pity on you, O Jerusalem,
> or who will bemoan you?
> Who will turn aside to ask about your welfare? (Jer 15:5)

Again, the poet speaks in a triad of rhetorical questions with clearly implied answers:

> *No one* will have pity on you (if Yʜwʜ does not);
> *No one* will bemoan you;
> *No one* will care about your *shalom*.

It is only Yʜwʜ who cares for Jerusalem and who will bring *shalom* to the city. Jerusalem is completely dependent on Yʜwʜ because there are no alternative agents who care or who will act. The ominous situation of Jerusalem is that the city, by its policies and by its conduct, has rejected its "only source of comfort and strength." And yet the text assumes and affirms that Yʜwʜ is indeed prepared to pity, to grieve, and to give *shalom* to the city, but not when rejected.

In the second text, Jeremiah 5:20–29, the poet addresses Jerusalem in its foolish recalcitrance. He does so, however, through an allusion to the power of the creator. It is the creator God who has "placed the sand as a boundary for the sea" (v. 22) – that is, who has set a limit to the threatening waters of chaos in order to create a safe space for creation. It is this chaos-curbing God who guarantees the rain and makes harvest regular and predictable (v. 24). Judah, among others, lives by the ordering power of the creator God.

Judah of all people should credit the creator God and respond in glad obedience.

Judah, however, is senseless, with eyes that do not see and ears that do not hear. Judah is stupid, foolish, and senseless in a death-choosing way. In any sensible trajectory, Judah would trust, fear, and obey YHWH. YHWH is astonished at the recalcitrance of Judah:

> Do you not fear me? says the LORD;
> Do you not tremble before me?
> I placed the sand as a boundary for the sea,
> a perpetual barrier that it cannot pass;
> though the waves toss, they cannot prevail,
> though they roar, they cannot pass over it. (Jer 5:22)

Again, rhetorical questions are offered with clear answers:

> *No,* Judah does not fear YHWH;
> *No,* Judah does not tremble before
> YHWH.

Judah imagines itself to be autonomous, not dependent on YHWH and therefore not needing to obey. This cynical disregard of YHWH the creator is rooted in a "stubborn and rebellious heart" (v. 23), expressed as greedy acquisitiveness (vv. 25–27). Had Judah reckoned with the creator, Judah would have known that the creator is committed to justice for the orphaned and the needy (v. 28). Thus, in characteristic fashion, the violation of the power and will of the creator God is made manifest in distorted neighbor relations that make viable society impossible. It is the creator God who sets limits on choice. But the aggressive scoundrels of Judah "know no limits." They surge wildly as chaotic waters and make life impossible on the terms of the creator God.

It is as though the creator God is astonished and appalled at this stubborn refusal of Judah. This poetic unit ends with two more rhetorical questions on the lips of the creator God, who expected to be feared by this peculiar people:

> Shall I not punish them?
> Shall I not bring retribution? (Jer 5:29)

On this point, Israel is no different from the nations. Both other nations and this special people live in the world of the creator God, who will not be mocked. And, when mocked, the creator God will act, whether against other nations or against beloved Judah. Either way, Yhwh will not be trifled with.

The final text I will cite with reference to Yhwh's incomparability is Jeremiah 30:21–22, the conclusion of the rhetorical unit of 30:18–22. This passage occurs in the "Book of Comfort," a collage of poetic passages concerning the restoration of Jerusalem. It is governed, characteristically, by the phrase, "restore the fortunes." In verse 18, this phrase bespeaks Yhwh's readiness to reverse the sorry condition of Jerusalem and bring it to new well-being. The passage anticipates full restoration, "as of old," with a promise to fend off any who would oppress Jerusalem (v. 20). It is asserted that the "prince" (*'addîr*) or "ruler" (*mōšēl*) will be one of them. This verse thus anticipates a restoration of monarchy but studiously avoids the term "king," allowing that Yhwh is the only real king in restored Jerusalem. The (new) prince will be "from them . . . from their midst"; that is, from among the Israelites as provided in Deuteronomy 17:15. Perhaps this phrasing envisions a displacement of foreign rulers imposed by Babylon. In any case, what interests us is the anticipation that this new ruler will "approach me" – that is, the ruler will function as did the ancient kings before the altar of Yhwh. The restoration will be fully complete; but we must not neglect the self-assertive comment of Yhwh, for who could dare approach Yhwh except those approved and invited by Yhwh to do so? Again, YHWH is no easy mark, is not readily available, but is an ominous access point that is carefully guarded. In giving access in such a demanding way, this God is incomparable, not like the gods who are flattered, bribed, and easily imposed on. There is a severity, even to the prince, that must be taken into account.

It is astonishing that the notion of severity moves to the covenant formula of verse 22, a formula often reiterated in the exilic literature:

> And you shall be my people,
> and I shall be your God. (Jer 30:22)

This God of *severe sovereignty* and *guarded access* wills a covenantal relationship with restored Israel. That possibility, however, is clearly and only at the behest of YHWH and on YHWH's own terms. *Thus even graciousness granted in exile is marked by incomparable sovereignty.* It is fair to say that all that unfolds in the Book of Jeremiah is an exposition of this claim of incomparability: a God powerful and gracious, a God who will not be mocked, a God who wills relationships but wholly on YHWH's own terms. Obviously, such an exposition of YHWH places the tradition of Jeremiah in deep tension with the Jerusalem ideology that imagined (and mediated) a more accommodating relationship with YHWH for the chosen people, the chosen king, and the chosen temple in the chosen city. The Book of Jeremiah keeps such generous chosenness constantly informed by the awesomeness of this God who is unmockable.

SOVEREIGNTY THROUGH PROPHECY

It is this YHWH – the incomparable God who governs in severity and fidelity, who will not be mocked, who wills a close relationship with the chosen people, the chosen city, the chosen dynasty, and the chosen temple – who occupies and dominates the Book of Jeremiah. It is this YHWH who is the key character and agent in the book. It is this *incomparable God* who is everywhere on the *pages of this book*. Because this God is incomparable, we might anticipate raw, direct enactment, and, if so, we are not disappointed. But because that raw, direct encounter is by means of the *pages of this book*, the encounter is mediated rather than immediate, proximate rather than direct.

The issue of mediating *God* through *pages* is a matter of immense concern to the Jewish tradition, so much so that establishing the authority of the *prophetic person* of Jeremiah and, by implication, the authority of the *prophetic book* of Jeremiah must receive primary attention. It is clear that this issue of prophetic authority is no incidental or secondary issue for the Jeremian tradition. Rather, it is a central problem and a central affirmation whereby these *pages* are offered (and received) in Israel as a mode of the person and activity of the incomparable *God*. In the Jeremian tradition, it is clear that without prophetic utterance and prophetic script, there can be no lively character and governing agency of YHWH. That the prophetic person and prophetic book can variously say "Thus saith the LORD" and "The LORD commanded me" serves to make the prophetic function integral to the way in which the incomparable God is known and met in and through these pages.

God's Sovereignty in the Prophetic Call

Jeremiah, both the person and the book, is the vehicle through which the incomparable God governs in general, and, more specifically, the vehicle through which God places the Jerusalem establishment in profound crisis. It is attested that Jeremiah is the one "to whom the word of the LORD came" (1:2). Unlike modern scholarship, the ancient tradition itself exhibits no interest in the psychological or sociological dimensions of this gift of the word. The witness is simply that the transmission of YHWH's word to Jeremiah was immediate and direct, thus giving authority to "the words of Jeremiah" that came to constitute the Book of Jeremiah (1:1).

This high claim for Jeremiah's authority as the one who can utter YHWH as key character and agent is the reason that the "call narrative" of the prophet is situated at the outset of the book (1:4–10).[6] This account of prophetic call offers the grounds for subsequent acceptance of the prophetic person and prophetic book as authoritative. This narrative – following a typical development – is dominated by YHWH's decisive verbs that place Jeremiah on the receiving end of the divine mandate. The verbs at the outset – formed, knew, consecrated, appointed – evoke in turn prophetic resistance (v. 6) and divine assurance (vv. 7–9). The narrative culminates in verse 10 with a second verb, "appoint" (*pqd*), to match the first "appoint" (*ntn*) in verse 5. In both cases, the prophetic mandate is "to the nations." It is clear in this scenario that Jeremiah is the recipient of divine address, is compelled to prophetic performance, and in fact is given no option.[7] Indeed, at the end, in verse 10, there is no response from Jeremiah; the final mandate of YHWH decidedly settles the matter.

This call narrative is commonly taken to be a reflection of the awesome experience of the prophetic person, Jeremiah. As interpretive interest has shifted to the prophetic book, however, it is credible to suggest that 1:4–10 is placed at the outset of the book in order to

---

[6] See Norman Habel, "The Form and Significance of the Call Narratives," *ZAW* 77 (1965): 297–323.

[7] See Brent A. Strawn, "Jeremiah's In/Effective Plea: Another Look at נצד in Jeremiah i 6," *VT* 55 (2005): 366–77.

give authority (primarily) to the entire Book of Jeremiah, whatever its historical provenance may have been. In canonical form, all of the Book of Jeremiah constitutes "the words of Jeremiah" (1:1), and all of it falls under the mandate of the powerful words of 1:10. It is clear that the prophetic book aims to redescribe and recharacterize the world of the nations, with Jerusalem as its pivot point, as an arena for Yhwh's decisive governance, a decisive governance character-istically ignored by the nations and characteristically domesticated by the Jerusalem establishment.

Although the tradition itself gives no hint of the "how" of the prophetic call, we may point to one concept that illuminates the call, namely "the divine council."[8] The notion of the divine council is a poetic image in the world of the Old Testament that concerns a convocation of many gods in heaven in order to determine the course of life on earth. In the monotheizing of the Old Testament, it is held that Yhwh presides over the assembly of subordinate gods, all of whom obey the "Chief God." Characteristically, the prophet is a human person dispatched to earth by the gods with messages about divine governance – thus the "messenger formula": "thus saith the Lord." This formula, recurrent in Jeremiah, attests that prophetic utterance is not the personal word of the prophet but is a divine message from a "higher authority."

Although it is not made explicitly clear that Jeremiah had access to the divine council, that image is important in the dismissal as phonies of prophets who rival Jeremiah. The competing prophets who contradict Jeremiah are said to be false because they have not

---

[8] See Patrick D. Miller, "Cosmology and World Order in the Old Testament: The Divine Council as Cosmic-Political Symbol," *HBT* 9 (1987): 53–78, and E. Theodore Mullen, *The Assembly of the Gods: The Divine Council in Canaanite and Hebrew Literature*, HSM 24 (Missoula, MT: Scholars Press, 1980).

been in the divine council and so they speak words that are not from God:[9]

> And the LORD said to me: The prophets are prophesying lies in my name; I did not send them, nor did I command them or speak to them. They are prophesying to you a lying vision, worthless divination, and the deceit of their own minds. (Jer 14:14)

> > I did not send the prophets, yet they ran;
> > I did not speak to them, yet they prophesied.
> > But if they had stood in *my council*,
> > then they would have proclaimed my words to my people,
> > and they would have turned them from their evil way,
> > and from the evil of their doings. (Jer 23:21–22)

Unlike these prophets, who are so readily dismissed, it is to be inferred that Jeremiah did indeed stand in the divine council, was sent by YHWH, and so speaks a true word (see 23:18). Thus it is clear that the words of Jeremiah (all of them that constitute the Book of Jeremiah) are words from YHWH that cannot be disregarded with impunity.

The divine intention communicated to Jeremiah is succinctly put in 1:10, which is something of a summary that will be exposited at great length in the Book of Jeremiah.[10] The prophet is given a twofold task. The negative task, given in four verbs – to pluck up and tear down, to destroy and overthrow – is to dismantle and destroy all that constitutes the Jerusalem establishment. Notice the sweeping formulation of the same point in 45:4, "the whole land."

---

[9] On the false prophets, see James L. Crenshaw, *Prophetic Conflict: Its Effect upon Israelite Religion*, BZAW 124 (Berlin: de Gruyter, 1971); and James A. Sanders, *From Sacred Story to Sacred Text: Canon as Paradigm* (Philadelphia: Fortress, 1987), 87–105.

[10] See Robert P. Carroll, *From Chaos to Covenant: Prophecy in the Book of Jeremiah* (New York: Crossroad, 1981), 55–58; and chapter 1 of the present book.

This task refers to the destruction of Jerusalem that happens – via Babylonian incursion – in the beginning of the sixth century. The second task given to the prophet is to "plant and build"; that is, to restore the Jerusalem that has been devastated, an anticipation that concurs with the latter part of the Book of Jeremiah, which is likely later than the person of Jeremiah. Thus the central mandate of the prophetic call concerns exactly the crisis of Jerusalem that is to be understood in terms of the governance of Yhwh that is articulated and enacted in the two steps of *judgment* and *restoration.*

It is to be observed concerning 1:10 that the prophet is to *effect* the destruction and the restoration, a theme that receives a variety of articulations in the poetry of the prophet. That is, Jeremiah's vocation is not simply to talk about, describe, report, or anticipate destruction and restoration but to enact all that by his utterance. Prophetic utterance is presented here as *performative*; the prophetic utterance performs what it says. Such a notion, of course, gives immense gravity to prophetic utterance, a gravity assigned it by the authorities who both trembled before that utterance and resented it deeply. Thus, by a careful reading of the call narrative, we conclude that the work of the prophet Jeremiah (and of the subsequent prophetic book) is to be the means whereby Yhwh as judge punishes Jerusalem and, as savior, restores Jerusalem. The prophet, both the person and the book, constitutes the way in which Yhwh exhibits governance over the city.

It is clear, particularly with reference to the first task of "plucking up and tearing down," that this material puts the prophet and the prophetic tradition in deep contradiction with the dominant theopolitical assumptions of Jerusalem. In the same way that Yhwh as judge is an unwelcome presence in the city, so the harsh utterances of the prophet are unwelcome. Thus, for example, Jeremiah is forbidden by Yhwh to intercede for the city, even though intercession was a primary practice of the prophets:

> The LORD said to me: Do not pray for the welfare of this people. Although they fast, I do not hear their cry, and although they offer burnt offering and grain offering, I do not accept them; but by the sword, by famine, and by pestilence I consume them. (Jer 14:11–12; see also 7:16; 11:14; 15:1)

This prohibition means that the connection of Israel (and Jerusalem) to Yhwh is broken; Yhwh will no longer be concerned with the need of Yhwh's people. Such a prophetic word places the city in profound crisis. It is therefore not surprising that the prophet in turn is placed in profound crisis for uttering and enacting a word that is unbearable in the city. It is that "word from the LORD" about "plucking up and tearing down" that stands at the center of prophetic identity. As a consequence, Jeremiah is variously opposed by "the men of Anathoth" (11:21–23), arrested by royal authorities (20:1–6), and dubbed a traitor by his contemporaries (38:4). The prophet, however, cannot do otherwise because the divine word to him is overpowering:

> Therefore thus says the LORD, the God of hosts;
> Because they have spoken this word,
> I am now making my words in your mouth a fire,
> and this people wood, and the fire shall devour them. (Jer 5:14)

> * * *

> If I say, "I will not mention him,
> or speak any more in his name,"
> then within me there is something like a burning fire
>   shut up in my bones;
> I am weary with holding it in, and I cannot. (Jer 20:9)

The unbearable word of Yhwh leads to the public rejection of the prophet. Rejected by the dominant community, the prophet is driven back to an abrasive interaction with Yʜᴡʜ, who is his only source of comfort and strength.

That abrasive intimacy is reflected in the "Lamentations of Jeremiah" that are taken by scholars to constitute a peculiar textual corpus that discloses the intense conflicted spiritual life of the prophet.[11] These prayers addressed to Yʜᴡʜ are reflective of the rhetoric of the Psalms, suggesting that the prophet is schooled in Israel's deepest, oldest liturgies.[12] In these prayers, the prophet petitions to Yʜᴡʜ for help and particularly petitions Yʜᴡʜ to take vengeance on his adversaries (Jer 12:1–4; 15:15–18; 17:18).[13] In light of the initial assurance to the prophet that Yʜᴡʜ would be with him (1:4–10), we might expect a response to prophetic petition in divine assurance. Instead, however, what is offered in divine response is an even greater divine command to be strong in the face of the hard task of utterance:

If you have raced with the foot-runners and they have wearied you,
how will you compete with horses?
And if in a safe land you fall down,
how will you fare in the thickets of the Jordan? (Jer 12:5)

* * *

Therefore thus says the Lᴏʀᴅ:
If you turn back, I will take you back,
and you shall stand before me.
If you utter what is precious, and not what is worthless,

---

[11] See Kathleen M. O'Connor, *The Confessions of Jeremiah: Their Interpretation and Their Role in Chapters 1–25*, SBLDS 94 (Atlanta: Scholars Press, 1987); A. R. Diamond, *The Confessions of Jeremiah in Context: Scenes of Prophetic Drama*, JSOTSup 47 (Sheffield: Sheffield Academic Press, 1987); and Mark S. Smith, *The Laments of Jeremiah and Their Contexts: A Literary and Redactional Study of Jeremiah 11–20*, SBLMS 42 (Atlanta: Scholars Press, 1990).

[12] See Walter Baumgartner, *Jeremiah's Poems of Lament* (Sheffield: Almond, 1988).

[13] On the struggle of the faith of the prophet, see H. Wheeler Robinson, *The Cross in the Old Testament* (Philadelphia: Westminster, 1955), 115–92.

you shall serve as my mouth.
It is they who will turn to you,
not you who will turn to them.
And I will make you to this people
a fortified wall of bronze;
they will fight against you,
but they shall not prevail over you,
for I am with you
to save you and deliver you, says the LORD. (Jer 15:19–20)

These prayers culminate in 20:7–13, a text that seems to run the gamut from anger at YHWH to confidence in YHWH and eventually, in verse 13, doxology to YHWH for having delivered the prophet. This utterance would be a fitting and appropriate culmination of this corpus if not for the fact that verses 7–13 are followed by verses 14–18, which articulate a profound negativity that is left unanswered and unresolved. It is obvious that the prophetic vocation that "plucks up and tears down" is indeed a nearly unbearable burden.

It is for that reason that the Lamentations of Jeremiah are subsumed under the topic of prophetic authority. The prophetic word given in this tradition, rooted in YHWH's own intentionality, is a massive refutation of the conventional faith of Jerusalem, a refutation that will lead, so says the tradition, to the destruction of the political-economic enterprise that is presumably grounded in divine assurance. Having said that, it is important to recognize that the critical judgments concerning these lamentations are complex and unresolved. The most obvious reading, the one offered here, is that these poems reflect the burden of the prophetic call. In some sense, however, the prayers are larger in scope than the prophetic person and attest to the travail of the community of Israel in its disputatious bonding with YHWH. Thus we must not read these poems simply as the voice of personal intimacy and anguish, for they, like everything else in Jeremiah, refer to a larger communal issue. Nonetheless, these prayers let us see, as Abraham J. Heschel has well noted, that the abrasive intimacy between God and prophet requires the prophets to experience and dwell in the grief and pathos of YHWH's own life over failed Jerusalem:

> Jeremiah depicted the dramatic tension in the inner life of God.... There were moments of compassion and moments of anger.... Again and again the prophet brought God's word to his beloved people: mourn, grieve, sorrow, lament.... These words [Jer 16:22, 26] are aglow with the divine pathos that can be reflected, but not pronounced: God is mourning Himself.... Israel's distress was more than a human tragedy. With Israel's distress came the affliction of God, his displacement, his homelessness in the land, in the world.[14]

Heschel sees how the deep tension in the inner life of YHWH is refracted in the life of the prophet, who must now embody all that is exposed and at risk for YHWH:

> This dialectic of what takes place in the prophetic consciousness points to the approach we have adopted in our analysis. Objectively considered, it is, on the one hand, the divine pathos that stirs and entices the prophet, and, on the other hand, unconditioned power that exercises sheer compulsion over the prophet. Subjectively, it is in consequence the willing response of sympathy to persuasion and also the sense of being utterly delivered up to the overwhelming power of God. A man whose message is doom for the people he loves not only forfeits his own capacity for joy, but also provokes the hostility and outrage of his contemporaries. The sights of woe, the anticipation of disaster, nearly crush his soul.[15]

> Jeremiah was called to an office both sublime and appalling. First he had to castigate, foretell doom and destruction; only after that could he comfort, offer hope, build and plant.[16]

---

[14] Abraham J. Heschel, *The Prophets* (New York: Harper and Row, 1962), 108–12.
[15] Ibid., 114.
[16] Ibid., 122–23.

As readers of the Book of Jeremiah, we may see how the man, and eventually the book, emerge in the midst of Israel as protest and alternative. The man and the book protest against a civic–sacred enterprise that is remote from the will of YHWH. They eventually voice an *alternative* because beyond destruction will come "planting and building." The prophet is the way in which YHWH – and the faith of Israel – experience the strange interface of divine purpose and Realpolitik. This odd, authorized prophetic voice shatters all the categories that keep divine reality separated from world reality. The two are here held together, bridged by a daring utterance, connected by the very body of the prophet who partakes of divine passion but who also lives amid worldly fear and anxiety. Quite clearly, the prophetic vocation enacted in this tradition precludes the Book of Jeremiah being taken according to any convenient categories of "theology" or "history." This book is indeed about a "strange new world" where the rule of God is palpable in a world that seems, on a mistaken reading, to be on its own.[17]

True versus False Prophecy

The poignancy of this prophetic tradition is made ever more stark when we recognize that this prophetic voice was vigorously contested along the way by "other prophets." In the canonical judgment of the Jeremian tradition, these other prophets are dismissed as "false"; in the dispute itself, however, it was not entirely clear which prophecy was true and which false.[18] The tradition of Jeremiah

---

[17] The reference is to Karl Barth, "The Strange New World Within the Bible," in his *The Word of God and the Word of Man* (New York: Harper and Row, 1957), 28–50.

[18] In addition to the studies of Crenshaw and Sanders cited in note 9 of this chapter, see Thomas W. Overholt, *The Threat of Falsehood: A Study in the Theology of the Book of Jeremiah*, SBT 16 (London: SCM, 1970).

stands opposed to a powerful strand of prophetic interpretation that was allied with the claims of dynasty and temple that saw YHWH as the sure guarantor of the city and its theological claims of legitimacy. We may cite four texts that exhibit this profound dispute.

First, Jeremiah 6:13–15 demonstrates that Jeremiah's opponents, schooled in the theological claims of the establishment, were sure of YHWH's generous guarantee of the well-being of the city:

> For from the least to the greatest of them,
> everyone is greedy for unjust gain;
> and from prophet to priest,
> everyone deals falsely.
> They have treated the wound of my people carelessly,
> saying, "Peace, peace," when there is no peace.
> They acted shamefully, they committed abomination;
> yet they were not ashamed,
> they did not know how to blush.
> Therefore they shall fall among those who fall;
> at the time that I punish them,
> they shall be overthrown, says the LORD. (Jer 6:13–15; see also 8:10–12)

The key issue for these voices is that Jeru*salem* is assured YHWH's *shalom*, and so nothing bad can ever happen there. Jeremiah sounds a counteropinion (counter to established claims) that there is no such thing as "guaranteed *shalom*." *All shalom* is conditional, and Jerusalem has failed to qualify for YHWH's *shalom* precisely because of ethical misconduct (greed and unjust gain) that violated the commands on which well-being rests.

It should be noted that this establishment motif of guaranteed *shalom* is rooted positively in the work of Isaiah a century earlier, for Isaiah had assured the well-being of Jerusalem:

> For I will defend this city to save it, for my own sake and for the sake of my servant David. (Isa 37:35)

In a less direct way and a century later, the voice of Jeremiah contradicts the claims of Isaiah. This is not to claim that Isaiah was wrong in his context but that "time makes ancient good uncouth." The prophet must speak a specific word in a specific context; his opponents are condemned because their ideological passion is remote from the true state of affairs with YHWH in the contemporary setting.

Second, the same condemnation of Jeremiah's opponents is sounded in Jeremiah 14:13–16. Because they have not been authorized or dispatched by YHWH, they offer a "lying vision" that is rooted not in the divine purpose but in the fantasy world of dominant Jerusalemite culture. In this condemnation, the tradition of Jeremiah thus contradicts not only specific prophetic voices but the entire theological program on which the Jerusalem establishment relied.

Third, the same critique is laid out in a more programmatic way in Jeremiah 23:9–22. This textual unit, with a formal title, "concerning the prophets," presents in systematic fashion the dispute of the Jeremian tradition with the interpretive propensity of prophets in Jerusalem allied with the royal temple ideology. The other prophets are condemned for "wickedness" (v. 11); for adultery and lies, whereby they "strengthen the hand of evildoers" (v. 14); and for speaking unauthorized words (v. 21). The imagery of the divine council is invoked with the clear inference to be drawn that Jeremiah, unlike his adversaries, had stood in the council of the gods and therefore speaks a true word. In verse 22, it is concluded that a "true word" would lead to repentance. Such repentance, however, depends on recognition that public life in Jerusalem is disobediently headed for disaster; these false prophets cannot utter such a hard declaration. It is evident that what is at stake is not simply the authority of Jeremiah, the Book of Jeremiah, or the tradition of Jeremiah. What is at stake, through prophetic utterance, is the contest of competing versions of public reality, one of which will lead to death for Jerusalem, not unlike the death of Sodom (v. 14). The life-giving alternative – offered by Jeremiah – leads to well-being. Such well-being, however, requires a radical departure from current public reality in the capital city.

Fourth, this programmatic dispute, so central to the Book of Jeremiah, is made specific through the narrative encounter in Jeremiah 27:16–28:17 between Jeremiah and Hananiah, a prophet in Jerusalem here declared false.[19] While we may accept Hananiah as a historical figure, it is clear that he also represents a "type" in the Book of Jeremiah, a type of prophet characteristically allied with the dominant power structure and not inclined to speak any word of critique against that power structure. The message of Hananiah after 598 BCE, after the first Babylonian incursion into the city, is that "within two years everything will return to normal" (Jer 28:3; see 27:16). Hananiah does not and cannot believe that the incursion by Babylon of 598 is serious and surely does not believe that it is the beginning of a larger scenario of devastation.

Hananiah is thus a proponent of a theology of Yhwh's generous protection and patronage for the holy city, its king, and its temple. Two observations about him may illuminate the dispute. First, his name means, quite literally, "Yhwh is gracious." This phrase became almost a mantra of the Jerusalem establishment, who believed that Yhwh's unconditional commitment to the city would preclude any harsh historical judgment. That is, Yhwh would fend off any serious military–political threat. This theology, in this period of Jerusalem's life, became an instance of

---

[19] On this narrative encounter, see Henri Mottu, "Jeremiah vs. Hananiah: Ideology and Truth in Old Testament Prophecy," in *The Bible and Liberation: Political and Social Hermeneutics*, ed. Norman K. Gottwald (Maryknoll, NY: Orbis, 1983), 235–51.

"cheap grace" that made YHWH into an undemanding patron of the city.

Second, it bears repeating that the conviction that YHWH would endlessly protect the city because YHWH is gracious is one that derives precisely from the prophet Isaiah a century earlier. It was Isaiah who declared that Jerusalem would be kept safe from the Assyrian threat.[20] Because the city was indeed delivered, seemingly miraculously, in 701 BCE, it became a trusted truism in Jerusalem that the city would remain safe. In this dispute, then, Jeremiah challenges not only Hananiah and his contemporary ilk who vainly imagine *shalom* in the city (6:14; 8:11), but an entire interpretive tradition rooted in the formidable authority of Isaiah. Jeremiah must assert that the well-grounded assurance from a century earlier no longer pertains because by now the city and its leadership have provoked YHWH to harshness that will not be curbed by "graciousness." The prophetic showdown in chapter 28 thus articulates a deep contest about faith, about the character of YHWH, and about the actual geopolitical circumstances of the city. In the event itself, one could not know who was right and who was wrong. But the narrative tradition of Jeremiah boldly asserts that there will be no quick return to normalcy. That conviction is vindicated, so far as this narrative is concerned, with the terse report that "Hananiah died" (28:17). In this narrative, the tradition surely intends to assert the truth of Jeremiah's severe message.

The Book: Beyond Jeremiah

We do not know when Jeremiah the prophet died. It seems clear, in any case, that the interpretive tradition of Jeremiah continued

---

[20] On the interpretive function of these texts in Isaiah, see Christopher R. Seitz, *Zion's Final Destiny: The Development of the Book of Isaiah: A Reassessment of Isaiah 36–39* (Minneapolis: Fortress, 1991).

to operate with vigor after the death of the prophet himself. Thus, while a great deal is staked on the prophet, his location, faith, and proclamation, the Book of Jeremiah moves past the person of Jeremiah in a continually energetic interpretive tradition. It is the current mood of scholarship to focus on the *book* rather than on the *man*, for the book seems to span several generations, certainly beyond the life span of the prophet. The continuing work of this tradition occurs in several seasons.

To begin with, life goes on. The community (or subcommunity) that valued Jeremiah's version of reality faced the vagaries of historical circumstance. After the razing of Jerusalem and the temple that was so passionately voiced by Jeremiah, the inhabitants of the city continued to live and face new historical circumstances. We learn variously that some continued to live in the environs of Jerusalem under a Jewish governor appointed by the occupying Babylonians (Jer 40:42). We also know that some fled (or were carried away) to Egypt (Jer 43:44). And we know that a most formidable subcommunity was deported and lived in Babylon (Jer 24). It was this latter subcommunity that is championed by the unfolding tradition of Jeremiah and that came to regard and assert itself as the true heirs and carriers of covenantal faith.[21] The outcome of a variety of historical, political, and military pressures produced a complex Jewish community that was dispersed and pluralistic. All of that surely lies beyond the horizon of the person of Jeremiah the prophet.

The emergence and growth of the Jeremian tradition happens surely because Yhwh, the Lord of history and the covenant Lord of Israel, continues to govern decisively in a variety of circumstances.

---

[21] It is entirely plausible that the inchoate beginnings of scribalism that are visible in the tradition of Jeremiah come to full and decisive fruition in the work of "Ezra the scribe." The continuity from *the prophetic* to *the scribal* is of immense importance for an understanding of the "rolling" character of the Book of Jeremiah.

If the prophet himself imagined that capitulation of Jerusalem to Babylon was Yʜᴡʜ's intention, then a later interpretive maneuver can, in its time, imagine that Yʜᴡʜ's will was the defeat and destruction of Babylon (Jer 50:51). While kingdoms rise and fall and the vagaries of public history move on, the abiding governance of Yʜᴡʜ through time, in time, and over time is a foundational conviction of this tradition.

The fact that life goes on and the claim that Yʜᴡʜ's rule abides through many circumstances together permit and require the interpretive tradition rooted in Jeremiah to be continually generative in the most imaginative ways. As this tradition can host the conviction that Yʜᴡʜ wills the termination of the city of Jerusalem, so the same interpretive tradition, later on in changed circumstances, can anticipate that Yʜᴡʜ wills the termination of imperial Babylon and the restoration of vulnerable Judah. It is important to see that the Book of Jeremiah has an extended interpretive trajectory beyond the devastation so focal for the prophet. Thus the ongoing *governing vitality of* Yʜᴡʜ has as its essential counterpart the ongoing *generative imagination of the interpretive tradition of Jeremiah.*

When we ask how it was that this tradition continued after the death of the prophet, it seems most plausible to suggest that the *prophetic tradition* of Israel was transposed into a *scribal practice*; consequently, the final form of the Book of Jeremiah is given not by the prophet but by his scribal heirs.[22] It is unmistakable on this score to note that the figure of Baruch the scribe is given great prominence in the Book of Jeremiah.[23] Indeed, Baruch the scribe is

---

[22] See the important, albeit tendentious, discussion of scribalism in Philip R. Davies, *Scribes and Schools: The Canonization of the Hebrew Scriptures,* LAI (Louisville, KY: Westminster John Knox, 1998).

[23] On the figure of Baruch, see James Muilenburg, "Baruch the Scribe," in *A Prophet to the Nations: Essays in Jeremiah Studies,* ed. Leo G. Perdue and Brian

alongside the prophet in the production of the scroll that became the book (36:4–19). Baruch, moreover, is instrumental in adding "many similar words" to the second version of the scroll (36:32). Baruch is deeply identified with the prophet and is identified in 43:3 as the one urging surrender to Babylon:

> But Baruch son of Neriah is inciting you against us, to hand us over to the Chaldeans, in order that they may kill us or take us into exile in Babylon. (Jer 43:3)[24]

Finally, in 45:4–5, Baruch is addressed in a special prophetic oracle promising that he will have his life "as a prize of war." (Note also his brother Seriah in the service of the prophetic tradition in 51:59–64.) I suggest that Baruch, historical person that he surely was, typifies the emergence of scribal practice, the purpose of which was to preserve in scrolls the old prophetic tradition and through interpretation extend the prophetic trajectory into new circumstances. Thus, without claiming more than the evidence permits, we may conclude that the Book of Jeremiah moves *beyond the man* via the scribal community that valued prophetic tradition and that extended prophetic traditions into new circumstances and that emerged as a dominant force in Judaism in the Persian period. We are able to see this in the way in which the final form of the Book of Jeremiah concerns not just the crises of 598 and 587 BCE on which the prophet concentrated but also the subsequent surviving community after the destruction, in the later Babylonian and into

W. Kovacs (Winona Lake, IN: Eisenbrauns, 1984), 229–45; and Richard Elliott Friedman, *Who Wrote the Bible?* (New York: Harper and Row, 1987), 146–49.

[24] See Walter Brueggemann, "The Baruch Connection: Reflections on Jeremiah 43:1–7," *JBL* 113 (1994): 405–20, reprinted in *Texts that Linger, Words that Explode: Listening to Prophetic Voices*, ed. Patrick D. Miller (Minneapolis: Fortress, 1999), 45–57.

the Persian periods. The prophetic tradition, rooted in Jeremiah, continued to be vibrant and credible and indeed definitional for the ongoing community.

A Prophet "Like Moses"

In the hands of the Deuteronomic editors of the Jeremian tradition, Deuteronomists who take the form of scroll-teaching scribes, Jeremiah is portrayed as the quintessential prophet "like Moses."[25] In Deuteronomy 18:15–21, the covenantal tradition of Deuteronomy anticipates a prophet to come who will be like Moses:

> The LORD your God will raise up for you a prophet like me from among your own people; you shall heed such a prophet. . . . I will raise up for them a prophet like you from among their own people; I will put my words in the mouth of the prophet, who shall speak to them everything that I command. (Deut 18:15, 18)

Although this text may anticipate a consecutive series of prophets (as, for example, in 2 Kings 17:13), William L. Holladay is correct in observing that the tradition characterizes Jeremiah exactly as the one "like Moses." Thus, in the Deuteronomic-scribal circles that brought the Book of Jeremiah to its final form, the connection between Moses and Jeremiah is a pivotal one and may suggest a particular instance of the conjunction of "the law and the prophets." What Moses had taught now comes to fruition in the words of Jeremiah.

It remains only to observe that the high claims made for the prophet Jeremiah – in the call narrative, in the "messenger

---

[25] See Christopher R. Seitz, "The Prophet Moses and the Canonical Shape of Jeremiah," *ZAW* 101 (1989): 3–27; and William L. Holladay, "The Background of Jeremiah's Self-Understanding: Moses, Samuel, and Psalm 22," *JBL* 83 (1964): 153–64.

formula," in the production of the scroll, and in the interaction with YHWH in the lamentations – now pertain not simply to the man Jeremiah but to the entire Book of Jeremiah. All of the book is presented as "the words of Jeremiah ... to whom the word of the LORD came" (1:1–2). This way of understanding prophetic authorization means that the later materials in the book that are clearly after the man are also (and nevertheless) to be understood as part of this contentious version of reality that is said to come from YHWH. The materials in the second and third generations after Jeremiah are also a prophetic word, in this case a word that will "plant and build." Taken as a dramatic whole, the Book of Jeremiah attests that it is YHWH's will that Judah must be "plucked up and broken down," but in the end it is "planting and building" after the abyss that prevails. All of this – the entire drama of YHWH's rule of the historical process – is indeed a word from the LORD.

YHWH'S SOVEREIGNTY AS JUDGMENT

For the tradition of Jeremiah, the die was cast in the first divine utterance in the theophany of Sinai:

> I am the LORD your God, who brought you out of the land of Egypt, out of the house of slavery; you shall have no other gods before me. (Exod 20:2–3)

YHWH's supreme sovereignty had been established and exhibited in the encounter with Pharaoh and the defeat of the Egyptian armies that signified the defeat of the Egyptian gods (Exod 12:12). There could be no legitimate rival for power, no competitor for legitimate authority. The entire covenantal tradition via the Deuteronomists had understood that Israel's relationship with YHWH depended on singular loyalty to this holy, jealous God that is evidenced in obedience to YHWH's commands.

While the Exodus narrative situates YHWH's victory and consequent authority vis-à-vis Egypt, in terms of Jeremiah the same matters obtain for false loyalties or self-securing autonomy. Both false loyalties (expressed as alliances) and autonomy constitute infringements on YHWH's singular exclusive authority, infringements that will not be tolerated. Such violations of legitimate authority evoke YHWH's effort to reestablish authority. That effort consists in juridical condemnation of the unfaithful partner and, where necessary, disciplinary sanctions that may be extremely violent. That violence is designed to reassert divine governance.

The prophetic task is to articulate this drama of divine sovereignty that is regularly challenged and reasserted, but always to do so vis-à-vis the geopolitical realities of the time. In the context of Jeremiah at the end of the seventh century BCE, the dominant geopolitical reality is Babylonian expansionism, the assertion of a new imperial power under Nebuchadnezzar, son of Nabopolassar, who founded the new regime. The two realities that Jeremiah confronted, then, are the *covenantal failure of Jerusalem* to be obedient and faithful to YHWH and the *threatening expansionism* of Babylon. To an outside observer, this theological claim and this political–military reality seem to have no transparent connection with each other. But this connection is exactly how prophetic faith works in the Old Testament. It connects *theological claim* and *public reality* and it does so, moreover, by an immense act of rhetoric, an act of what I have termed "prophetic imagination."[26]

---

[26]Walter Brueggemann, *The Prophetic Imagination*, 2nd ed. (Minneapolis: Fortress, 2001).

Consequently, the Book of Jeremiah may be understood as a long, sustained act of prophetic imagination whereby theological claim and political reality are shown to be intrinsically related. The connection between the two in the tradition of Jeremiah is made through vigorous and daring rhetorical ventures, a rhetoric that moves easily and compellingly between theological claim and public reality. Thus, primary attention in the study of the prophets need not focus on historical context but rather on the rhetorical inventiveness that makes these connections. (The historical context is important, but it can be seen quickly in broad strokes and for our purposes, need not be probed, in excessive detail.)

By the end of the seventh century BCE, in something of a culmination of the prophetic trajectory, the covenantal–Deuteronomic–prophetic tradition had concluded that Jerusalem was in serious breach of its covenant with YHWH, a breach so serious that the survival of the urban regime was in great jeopardy. That jeopardy was grounded in YHWH's wrathful assault on a covenant partner who had defaulted on the relationship. As a consequence, Jeremiah, as a seventh-century spokesperson for this covenant, is summoned by divine compulsion to the prophetic task of "plucking up and breaking down, of destroying and overthrowing (1:10; see also 11:1 –8). The intention (and effect?) of this rhetoric of judgment is to exhibit the failure, dismantling, and demise of the Jerusalem establishment and to employ rhetoric that is artistic and powerful enough that the listener can, in the very hearing, experience the failure and soon-to-come dismantling and demise of the beloved city. The rhetoric is a vehicle whereby the fierce sovereignty of YHWH, in the face of challenge, is vigorously reasserted over a recalcitrant covenant partner.

Jeremiah's rhetoric of divine judgment roughly exhibits the general form of what scholars have come to call a "speech of judgment," or alternatively a "prophetic judgment-speech."[27] The speech of judgment, in seemingly limitless variations, consists of two major parts, an *indictment* that specifies the way in which the covenant people has violated the covenant and a *sentence* that specifies the punishment to be given for the violation. On the one hand, both indictment and sentence are deeply rooted in tradition. The indictment concerns violation of the covenant or, more exactly, of covenant stipulations. The sentence anticipates the implementation of a covenantal sanction (curse).[28] Although this form of speech is clear and well established, an imaginative poet like Jeremiah can generate a wide range of variations in terms of image and metaphor through which failure and punishment can be voiced. Characteristically, the indictment leads to a sentence; allowance is sometimes made, however, for the failed party to repent of failed behavior and so avert the impending punishment. If there is no such repentance or if the repentance is too little too late, the prophetic rhetoric insists that the punishment, judged to be appropriate to the case, may be extreme and intense, such extremity leading to the termination of the failed party. In much of Jeremiah, the anticipated judgment is harsh, violent, and extreme. Although such harshness cannot be explained away, it is at any rate useful to remember that such divine harshness is in the context of a betrayed relationship. The extremity of divine anger is commensurate with the affront that violates the

---

[27] On the genre, see Claus Westermann, *Basic Forms of Prophetic Speech* (Philadelphia: Westminster, 1967).

[28] Notice should be taken of the conventional list of curses given in Jeremiah in various configurations: "pestilence, sword, family" and sometimes "captivity" (Jer 14:12; 15:2; 24:10; 27:8, 13; 28:8; 29:17–18; 32:24, 36; 34:17; 38:2; 44:13). See Delbert R. Hillers, *Treaty-Curses and the Old Testament Prophets*, BibOr 16 (Rome: Pontifical Biblical Institute, 1964).

covenant.[29] The typical articulation of the lawsuit form signi-
fies that from Yhwh's perspective (the perspective voiced by the
prophet) Israel's conduct has so deeply contradicted Yhwh's intentions that only a sorrowful end for Israel (and for the covenant) is
imaginable. Whereas such judgment is sometimes taken to be disciplinary and aimed at a restorable relationship, in the Jeremian corpus it is not obvious that the speeches of judgment aim at restoration. Very often, the rhetoric moves in the direction of termination
because this sovereign God will not be mocked.

Before taking up particular texts concerning the divine judgment
of Jerusalem, we may pause to consider the peculiarity of the aim
and effect of prophetic rhetoric, "namely" to connect divine purpose and divine resolve to Realpolitik. In the ancient world, it was
possible – not easy, of course, but possible – to imagine that the
public world of geopolitics was autonomous and without divine
governance. Such a claim would not have been made frontally in
the ancient world. Rather, it would have been accomplished by the
assumption that God exercised no real authority or power to affect
anything:

> At that time I will search Jerusalem with lamps,
> and I will punish the people
> who rest complacently on their dregs,
> those who say in their hearts,
> "The Lord will not do good,
> nor will he do harm." (Zeph 1:12)

Against that notion of divine indifference or irrelevance, the
prophetic tradition in general and the Jeremian tradition in particular insist on the *real agency* of Yhwh in public affairs, a hidden

[29] See Patrick D. Miller, Jr., *Sin and Judgment in the Prophets*, SBLMS 27 (Chico,
CA: Scholars Press, 1982).

governance that Klaus Koch terms "suprahistory" or "meta-history" – a hidden governance only made visible and recognizable through prophetic utterance.[30] These prophetic speeches of judgment make visible the claim that political practice contradicts divine intention and is subject to divine sanction. Even in the ancient world of political arrogance, the assertion of divine agency is a daring rhetorical act. How much more so in the modern world where secular assumptions prevail!

In his excellent study *The Rise and Fall of the Great Powers*, Paul M. Kennedy has proposed a taxonomy whereby great powers collapse when military expenditures skew the economy.[31] As a social scientist, Kennedy, of course, makes no explicit moral or theological judgment on such a "fall." It occurs to me, however, that Kennedy's careful calculus is not far removed from ancient prophetic reasoning. Both share the conviction that there are hidden, intractable limits beyond which arrogant, autonomous power becomes self-destructive. Kennedy, of course, makes his claim without reference to divine agency. In Jeremiah, by contrast, divine agency is central to the rhetoric. YHWH is the first-person subject of the great verbs of "plucking up and pulling down." YHWH is the agent before whom the leadership in Jerusalem (or in Babylon) is dramatically helpless. These prophetic articulations of judgment are remarkable acts of rhetoric designed not only to state the "facts of the case" but to make an affective appeal whereby the listening community can participate in the reality of divine action that is disclosed in prophetic utterance.

---

[30] Koch, *The Prophets I*, 5, 73, 88, 99, 121, 144, and passim.

[31] Paul M. Kennedy, *The Rise and Fall of the Great Powers: Economic Change and Military Conflict from 1500 to 2000* (New York: Random House, 1987).

With this background in place, I will consider six exemplary cases in which poetic rhetoric enunciates the judgment of YHWH on Jerusalem. The primal claim of judgment assumes that YHWH is in the right;[32] even so, primary attention should be paid to the way in which the rhetoric works, thereby making the flat claim of judgment available to the imagination of Israel.

YHWH: *Scorned Spouse*

Following the imagery of Hosea, YHWH is presented as an affronted marriage partner who punishes the unfaithful partner.[33] After the call narrative of Jeremiah 1:4–10 that legitimates the prophetic person and the prophetic book, and after the related materials of 1:11–19, the first poems in the Book of Jeremiah place Jerusalem under judgment according to the image of marital infidelity (2:1– 37; 3:1–4:4). At the outset, YHWH can remember the initial passion of the covenantal relationship in which Israel was a smitten, adoring bride (2:2). Very soon, however, the relationship went awry: The bride who "followed" YHWH (2:2) now "went after" other lovers (2:5) and abandoned YHWH in disobedience (2:6–8). In the extended poem that follows, this marital imagery is treated in a quite expansive way. The main point of indictment, however, is constant: Israel has "forsaken" YHWH (2:13–17, 19) – that is, Israel

---

[32] This is a recurring assumption of the prophets. It is countered in the lament psalms that accuse YHWH as the one who has violated the covenant. See Psalm 44 as a classic example of this claim.

[33] On the problem of such rhetorical violence, see Carol J. Dempsey, *The Prophets: A Liberation-Critical Reading* (Minneapolis: Fortress, 2000); Regina M. Schwartz, *The Curse of Cain: The Violent Legacy of Monotheism* (Chicago: University of Chicago Press, 1997); and Renita J. Weems, *Battered Love: Marriage, Sex, and Violence in the Hebrew Prophets*, OBT (Minneapolis: Fortress, 1995).

has walked out on the marriage. Israel did this by seeking other lovers, other loyalties both religious and political. The poetic strategy of this poem is to situate the infidelity of Israel on the very lips of Israel by Israel's own avowal:

I will not serve! (Jer 2:20)

* * *

I am not defiled,
I have not gone after the Baals (Jer 2:23)

* * *

You are my father.... You gave me birth.... Come and save us! (Jer 2:27)

* * *

We are free, we will come to you no more. (Jer 2:31)

* * *

I am innocent; surely his anger has turned from me.... I have not sinned. (Jer 2:35)

The sum of the whole is Israel's refusal to honor the covenantal/marital commitments she has made to YHWH.

Such infidelity evokes the scornful anger of YHWH, who is not only a sovereign but a betrayed, shamed lover who goes nearly berserk in rage.[34] The punishment for such infidelity takes place in the public domain as the poetry moves beyond the primal metaphor. Hence, we hear that Egypt has invaded and abused the land (2:16). The poetry anticipates that Israel will be shamed as a result:

---

[34] The extreme form of such divine rage is in the narrative recitals of Ezekiel 16:37–43 and 23:22–49.

> As a thief is shamed when caught,
> so the house of Israel shall be shamed –
> they, their kings, their officials,
> their priests, and their prophets. (Jer 2:26)

The leadership will be humiliated and exhibited as a failure. The shame will come via the assault of the political–military apparatus of Egypt and Assyria (2:36). The final verse of the poem suggests deportation, as God's people will be broken and humiliated "from there" (2:37).

The same imagery of marital infidelity proceeds in a different way in 3:1–4:4. This poem begins with an allusion back to the Torah commandment of Deuteronomy 24:1–4. As Michael Fishbane has shown, the prophetic poem transposes a commandment into a most suggestive metaphor.[35] The poem begins by identifying "a man," who is YHWH; "his wife," who is Israel; and "another man," who is the false gods who are alternatives to YHWH. The old teaching of Moses made it impossible for such a wayward wife to return to her first husband. In the context of Jeremiah, this means that wayward Israel cannot return to YHWH after "sleeping around" with other gods. The reason there may be no return is that the woman "Israel" has been "defiled" by the second relationship. This disloyalty, which in context has clear sexual dimensions, creates ritual uncleanness whereby the other relationship is voided and the land is placed in jeopardy. The point of using Deuteronomy 24:1–4 is to preclude a return to the first husband. The affronted husband, moreover, is the rainmaking God who brings a devastating drought on fickle people (3:3–5). Thus, the punishment is severe and calibrated to correspond to the affront.

---

[35] Michael Fishbane, *Biblical Interpretation in Ancient Israel* (Oxford: Clarendon, 1985), 307–12.

What astonishes us in the poetic verses that follow is that Yhwh, against the commandment of Moses in Deuteronomy, wills the faithless covenant partner Israel to come home. Yhwh, in this poem, is willing to override the Torah for the sake of the relationship. It is this willingness on the part of Yhwh that provides the impetus in the Book of Jeremiah for restoration after devastation, thus the bid for return:

> Return, faithless Israel,
> says the Lord.
> I will not look on you in anger,
> for I am merciful,
> says the Lord;
> I will not be angry forever. (Jer 3:12)

* * *

> Return, O faithless children, says the
> Lord,
> for I am your master;
> I will take you, one from a city and two
> from a family,
> and I will bring you to Zion. (Jer 3:14)

* * *

> Return, O faithless children,
> I will heal your faithlessness.
> "Here we come to you;
> for you are the Lord our God." (Jer 3:22)

To be sure, there is anger evoked by the defilement. The primary mood of the poetry, however, is wistful sadness. Thus, in 3:19 we are given a poetic glimpse into the pain and disappointment of Yhwh, who had expected more from Israel but now sees its profound faithlessness (3:20).

The way is nonetheless open for a return to Yʜwʜ and the restoration of the relationship. Such a return, however, is not an easy one; it requires fidelity to Yʜwʜ's primal passions:

> If you return, O Israel,
> says the Lᴏʀᴅ,
> if you return to me,
> if you remove your abominations
> from my presence,
> and do not waver,
> and if you swear, "As the Lᴏʀᴅ lives!"
> in truth, in justice, and in uprightness,
> then nations shall be blessed by him,
> and by him they shall boast. (Jer 4:1–2)

Thus the prophetic accent on truth, justice, and uprightness sounds all around the sadness and the wistful yearning for restoration.

Sadness and wistfulness constitute an uncommonly poignant motif in Jeremiah's exposition of the covenant. The metaphor of marriage draws the listening community back behind the more formal motifs of *judicial propriety* into intense interpersonal relationships that are saturated with passion and pathos.[36] What is at stake here is not a formal relationship but a deeply felt intimacy that is jeopardized and then forfeited. The poetry makes clear that Yʜwʜ is not just an affronted ruler but a weary lover who suffers in the alienation. Furthermore, it is this suffering of the wounded lover that becomes the ground for hope in the tradition of Jeremiah and the ground for looking beyond devastation and alienation. Following in the wake of Hosea, Jeremiah has boldly recast the covenant faith of Israel in categories of passion and

---

[36]On this movement, see Heschel, *The Prophets.*

intense intimacy. The divine lover is capable of immense affection and, not surprisingly, deeply felt indignation and humiliation that arise out of betrayal. The function of such intimate pathos-filled poetry is to draw the reader into the affective reality of Yhwh's judgment.

Yhwh: *Provoked and Punishing Sovereign*

Yhwh is presented as a provoked sovereign who punishes a recalcitrant vassal state by deploying rapacious military troops against it. In an abrupt change of mood and rhetoric, chapters 4–6 offer a series of poems concerning military invasion (4:5–8, 13–18, 29–31; 5:6, 14–17; 6:1–8, 22–25). The rhetoric of these poems only occasionally identifies Yhwh as the agent who mobilizes the assaulting army and dispatches it against Jerusalem:

> Raise a standard toward Zion,
> flee for safety, do not delay,
> for I am bringing evil from the north,
> and a great destruction. (Jer 4:6)

* * *

> I am going to bring upon you a nation from far away,
> O house of Israel, says the Lord.
> It is an enduring nation,
> it is an ancient nation,
> a nation whose language you do not know,
> nor can you understand what they say. (Jer 5:15)

Most often, the poems articulate both a characterization of the ominousness of the invading armies and the alarm and fear that are evoked by the coming military threat. But even where Yhwh's direct agency is not stated, it is clearly implied. Everywhere in this poetry it is unmistakably clear that Yhwh has declared war on Yhwh's own people and own city and has unleashed a mighty force that is irresistible in its devastation. In the poetry itself, we are given no hint at the identity of the coming army, for the characterization could pertain to any invading army:

> It is an enduring nation,
> it is an ancient nation,
> a nation whose language you do not know,
> nor can you understand what they say.
> Their quiver is like an open tomb;
> all of them are mighty warriors. (Jer 5:15b–16)

* * *

> Thus says the LORD:
> See, a people is coming from the land of the north,
> a great nation is stirring from
> the farthest parts of the earth.
> They grasp the bow and the javelin,
> they are cruel and have no mercy,
> their sound is like the roaring sea;
> they ride on horses,
> equipped like a warrior for battle,
> against you, O daughter Zion! (Jer 6:22–23)

In the context of the Book of Jeremiah, of course, the enemy is clearly Babylon, the great imperial force that came against the city and devastated it. Thus, the simple story line is that Yhwh *dispatches Babylon* to punish Israel as a disobedient people. This single story line is appropriate both in terms of its bold theological claims and in terms of the affective force of the rhetoric, as well as reflecting the Realpolitik of the seventh–sixth centuries BCE.

Almost without calling attention to it, this poetry proceeds in the conviction that Yhwh as sovereign presides over *the entire international scene*; Yhwh can summon and dispatch great armies and great states to accomplish the divine purpose. In this particular case, the poetry makes the breathtaking claim that mighty Babylon, a great nemesis to Jerusalem, is *the tool and vehicle for the divine purpose*. It could of course be possible to understand the Babylonian push into Israel and Judah in terms of Realpolitik, without reference to the divine purpose. Such a reading, however, is remote from and irrelevant to the Book of Jeremiah; the prophet has no interest in strategic explanations but is concerned with making clear that the sovereign God presides over the affairs of all nations and can dispatch a *goy*-nation in a way that touches the privileged position of Israel. The dispatch of the invading army functions as the *sentence* of prophetic utterance. The *indictment* in this textual unit that lies behind the *sentence* is stated only incidentally. It concerns disregard of the Torah (5:4), the abuse of the poor and vulnerable (5:26–28), and greed based on self-deception (6:13–14). The daring of prophetic theology is that it makes a decisive connection between *social disarray* and *international military deployment*, holding the two together as an expression of the divine purpose and authority.

The affective domain of the poem is designed so that the listening community may embrace the immense jeopardy that follows disobedience. For example, in 4:19–20, the poetry characterizes the heart-stopping shock when an invading army comes into one's tent and one is helpless before the violence; or, in 6:4 there is a bid for civil defense preparation. But the cry "Woe to us" indicates that the inhabitants of Jerusalem are portrayed as lacking resources or wisdom for the emergency. The poetry makes apparent the complete helplessness of the people of God, who stand exposed before the ire enacted by YHWH. Most poignantly, the poetic unit of 4:29–31 voices the extreme danger in which the city stands. Before the clatter of racing invaders, the local inhabitants head for the hills in a panic (4:29). In the midst of the panic, however, one figure – in the imagination of the poet – does not flee but remains on the street, perhaps believing that she has enough wiles to stay the threat. This lone figure that did not flee – "And you, O desolate one" (4:30) – is perhaps Jerusalem at its most obdurate and self-willed. This one – the city – stays on the streets and presents herself as a prostitute ready to welcome the coming soldiers, dressed in crimson and ornaments of gold, with large, painted eyes. Without overstating the case, the poetry labels the city of Jerusalem as a whore who believes she has the capacity to tame the military threat. But that is nothing more than a long-standing urban legend. Verse 31 makes clear that such posturing in self-confidence is completely futile and no help at all. The imagery shifts promptly to that of a desperately abused and abandoned woman who is now left helpless in the violence of the street:

> For I heard a cry as of a woman in labor,
> anguish as of one bringing forth her first child,
> the cry of daughter Zion gasping for breath,
> stretching out her hands,
> "Woe is me! I am fainting before killers!" (Jer 4:31)

Her self-confidence is broken. She gasps, begs for help, reaches out for rescue, of which there is none. All she can finally say is, "Woe is me." This is nothing more than an imaginative, prophetic poem. But the poem in its almost unbearable rhetorical power communicates the complexity and jeopardy of life where YHWH rules. YHWH, of course, is remote from the crime on the street. But all that is, nevertheless, at the behest of YHWH. The Babylonian armies serve only to enforce divine severity. At the moment, it is easier for YHWH to rule in Babylon than in Jerusalem. YHWH, moreover, will not quit until YHWH's order is fully reestablished in Jerusalem. The people and the city are under assault, and there is nowhere to hide in safety. The invaders show "no mercy," and that is because the God who sends them, in this moment, is also without mercy (see 6:22–23).

Yʜwʜ: *Powerful Healer*

Yʜwʜ is presented as a powerful healer who can restore what is broken and diseased; in this particular case, however, Yʜwʜ is either unable or unwilling to heal Jerusalem, a city that is terminally ill and must die. Since the Exodus event, the wonder of deliverance has been understood as a great miraculous healing from "the diseases of Egypt":

> He said, "If you will listen carefully to the voice of the Lᴏʀᴅ your God, and do what is right in his sight, and give heed to his commandments and keep all his statutes, I will not bring upon you any of the diseases that I brought upon the Egyptians; for *I am the* Lᴏʀᴅ *who heals you.*" (Exod 15:26; see also Deut 28:27)

Yʜwʜ is indeed the doctor:

> ... who forgives all your iniquity,
> who *heals all your diseases*,
> who redeems your life from the Pit,
> who crowns you with steadfast love and mercy,
> who satisfies you with good as long as you live
> so that your youth is renewed like the eagle's. (Ps 103:3–5)

Jeremiah is, moreover, informed by the tradition of Hosea who testifies to the healing capacity of Yʜwʜ:

> Come, let us return to the Lᴏʀᴅ;
> for it is he who has torn, and
> *he will heal us*;
> he has struck down, and he
> will bind us up.
> After two days he will revive us;
> on the third day he will raise us up,
> that we may live before him. (Hos 6:1–2)

In the case of Jeremiah, however, the extremity of Israel's disability is so acute that even the traditional confidence in Yʜwʜ as physician is now inadequate. The text of Jeremiah 8:18–9:3 portrays

Yhwh as the one who stands by helplessly, grieving over Jerusalem's diseased state but unable to do anything to counter the deathliness that has gathered around the city. Yhwh speaks grief while observing the condition of "my people." The poem is dominated by the thrice-used phrase "my poor people" or, alternatively, "my dear people" (vv. 19, 21, 22).[37] This terminology bespeaks Yhwh's intense link to and concern for Jerusalem. The immense grief of Yhwh in verse 18 is matched by the emotive response of 9:1 wherein Yhwh's eyes become fountains of tears. Given the verdict of verse 18 and the refrain in verse 21, verses 19–20 allude to the complaint spoken in the Jerusalem liturgy, a complaint about Yhwh's absence and the deathliness that was its consequence. Thus, in verse 19, Israel wonders if Yhwh is present at all as a saving presence in the temple:

> Hark, the cry of my poor people
> from far and wide in the land:
> "Is the Lord not in Zion?
> Is her King not in her?"
> ("Why have they provoked me to
> anger with their images,
> with their foreign idols?") (Jer 8:19)

In verse 20, Israel recognizes the expected time of healing has passed without any miracle:

The harvest is past, the summer is ended,
and we are not saved. (Jer 8:20)
Verse 22 is dominated by three questions, the answer to which is in
    dispute.[38]
Is there no balm in Gilead?

---

[37] Jack R. Lundbom, in his *Jeremiah 1–20: A New Translation with Introduction and Commentary*, AB 21 A (New York: Doubleday, 1999), 537, proposes the latter attractive reading.

[38] See Walter Brueggemann, "Jeremiah's Use of Rhetorical Questions," *JBL* 92 (1973): 358–74.

Is there no physician there?
Why then has the health of my poor people
not been restored? (Jer 8:22)

One may, with Jack R. Lundbom, say of the first two questions
that a positive answer is intended. Yes, there is balm; yes, there
is a doctor. The positive answers to the first two questions would
then ironically assert the negative response to the third question.
Alternatively, one may imagine a *negative* answer for the first two
questions: "No, no balm . . . no, no doctor." Either way, the accent
is on the third question in verse 22:

why then . . . not restored?

Why no healing? If we follow the tradition of the positive answer
to the first two questions, then the third question is intended as a
rhetorical jolt; what is possible is not, in this moment, available.
Perhaps the sickness is too far advanced, perhaps the sickness is
merited by Israel's disobedience, or perhaps Yhwh is unconcerned.
We are not told. What is clear is that there is no healing, and so the
suffering illness becomes more acute, even to death. And Yhwh can
only grieve (9:1). Even Yhwh cannot intervene to save. The disease
is too far along, and Yhwh must knowingly give up beloved Israel
to the power of death. Yhwh cannot or will not save. Either way,
the end result is the same.

The use of the image of sickness is not extensive; it is, however, enough to imagine that Jerusalem is on a slide toward death.
In this case, judgment is not a direct initiative taken by Yhwh.
Rather, the sickness is intrinsic to the circumstance Jerusalem has
designed for itself. The disease will work its way through the body
politic. The outcome is not in doubt. Israel will die in its disobedience. In the text, the patient is beyond help. There has been no

healing because Israel has ranged so far away from what is normal that there is no divine reach toward the suffering. This rhetoric is of interest because Yнwн exercises no agency. Rather, the judgment is "in the cards," in the very processes of life itself.[39] Yнwн is the guarantor of those processes so that consequences follow deeds, illness follows disobedience, and death follows acute disobedience. But Yнwн is portrayed not as an agent of wrath but as a helpless, aggrieved observer of a death that Yнwн does not desire.

Yнwн: Creator of Order

Yнwн is portrayed as the creator God who orders and maintains a visible, coherent fabric of life that produces well-being in which that order is honored. Israel, however, lacks the wisdom to conform to the divine order of creation, which is not negotiable. Lacking wisdom, Israel engages in self-destruction through its foolish disregard of life's elemental ordering. This *foolishness kills!*[40] As with the imagery of healing, in this imagery, Yнwн is no active agent of Israel's punishment but only the guarantor of a system of "deeds and consequences" that leave death and termination as the inescapable outcome of foolishness. A number of texts appeal to what may be termed "wisdom theology," in which Yнwн is primally the orderer of a life system.[41]

---

[39] This way of understanding divine judgment has been explicated in Klaus Koch, "Is There a Doctrine of Retribution in the Old Testament?" in *Theodicy in the Old Testament*, ed. James L. Crenshaw, IRT 4 (Philadelphia: Fortress, 1983), 47–87.

[40] Gerhard von Rad, *Wisdom in Israel* (Nashville, TN: Abingdon, 1972), 65, nicely calls such foolishness "practical atheism."

[41] See Lennart Boström, *The God of the Sages: The Portrayal of God in the Book of Proverbs*, ConBOT 29 (Stockholm: Almqvist and Wiksells, 1990).

In 5:4–5, the "poor" are condemned as "foolish." This foolishness is a failure to attend to "the way of Yʜᴡʜ." The "rich" are likewise condemned because they also lack knowledge of the justice of God. They are recalcitrant in their autonomy and will be destroyed:

> But they all alike had broken the yoke,
> they had burst the bonds. (Jer 5:5c,d)

The house of Jacob and Judah is condemned in 5:20–24 because this is a people "foolish and without heart" who disregard the "boundaries" of creation and so invite chaos on themselves:

> Do you not fear me? says the Lᴏʀᴅ;
> Do you not tremble before me?
> I placed the sand as a boundary for the sea,
> a perpetual barrier that it cannot pass;
> though the waves toss, they cannot prevail,
> though they roar, they cannot pass over it.
> (Jer 5:22)

This disregard by Jerusalem of the order of creation eventuated in the exploitation of the orphans and widows (Jer 5:26–28). Indeed, the people of Jerusalem do not even acknowledge that Yʜᴡʜ is the giver of rain that makes life possible:

> They do not say in their hearts,
> "Let us fear the Lᴏʀᴅ our God,
> who gives the rain in its season,
> the autumn rain and the spring rain,
> and keeps for us
> the weeks appointed for the harvest." (Jer 5:24)

This rhetoric that appeals to the reliable, life-giving processes of creation shrewdly links *the order of creation* to *the disorder of society* through acquisitiveness. Foolishness about the givenness of creation results in destructive foolishness concerning social policy and social conduct.

The indictment of 8:7 contrasts the inherent wisdom of migrating birds with the lack of such wisdom on the part of Israel. The contrast indicates that Israel lacks elemental knowledge of the "ordinance of YHWH"; it rejects such knowledge in its penchant for self-destruction. In verses 8–9, the entire claim of "wisdom" in Israel, especially that of deceived scribes, is dismissed as destructive foolishness.

In 17:11, the unjustly wealthy in Jerusalem are "proved to be fools." Their wealth is as inappropriate to them as are the eggs a partridge hen hatches that she did not lay. This image, like that of the migrating birds, indicts Israel for "unnatural" action that is contrary to its true character as YHWH's primal partner.

Yet a third appeal to "nature" is in 18:15–16. It is not "natural" for the snows of Lebanon to melt; it is not "natural" for mountain streams to run dry. So also it is not "natural" for Israel to forget YHWH. But Israel has forgotten through its own disobedience:

> But my people have forgotten me,
> they burn offerings to a delusion;
> they have stumbled in their ways,
> in the ancient roads,
> and have gone into bypaths,
> not the highway. (Jer 18:15)

In all of these cases, Israel self-destructs by means of a foolishness that runs against the grain of YHWH's created order. This foolishness of disobedience creates its own "sphere of destiny"; that is, a sphere of death. According to this rhetoric, the final outcome – death – is inevitable.

YHWH: God of Life and God of Death

YHWH is known to be the God of life (Jer 10:10). But now, in prophetic rhetoric, the God of life stands passive while the reality of death surges on Israel. There is in this rhetoric no speculation about the power of death, though it is readily inferred that such deathliness is a tool of YHWH's sovereignty. Jeremiah's rhetoric of grief is not designed to explain; rather, its aim is to summon the listening community to enter into its destiny, to experience what is in fact happening, even in the face of powerful denial.

Thus, the prophet utters a poem that summons Israel to grieve over a drought that will devastate the land and immobilize the urban economy:

> Take up weeping and wailing
> for the mountains,
> and a lamentation for the
> pastures of the wilderness,
> because they are laid waste so
> that no one passes through,
> and the lowing of cattle is not heard;
> both the birds of the air and the animals
> have fled and are gone.
> I will make Jerusalem a heap of ruins,
> a lair of jackals;
> and I will make the towns of
> Judah a desolation,
> without inhabitant. (Jer 9:10–11)

The crisis is so acute that the "professional" woman grievers are to be mobilized (9:17). The poem anticipates a great public crisis in which the loss in the community is immense and can no longer be denied:

> For a sound of wailing is heard from Zion:
> "How we are ruined!
> We are utterly shamed,
> because we have left the land,
> because they have cast down our dwellings. (Jer 9:19)

The agency of such misery is "death" as an invasive force. It is inescapable, however, that the intrusion of death is dispatched by YHWH. It is of course YHWH "who kills and makes alive" (1 Sam 2:6). And now this God of life has turned the city into an arena of death. The imagery, anticipatory of the vivid scenes of Auschwitz, is of corpses piled high, the outcome of terror unleashed against a recalcitrant city (Jer 9:22; see 7:32–33).

YHWH: Angry and Unrestrained

YHWH is portrayed as particularly aligned in anger against the power structure of Jerusalem. The very leaders who were to act on behalf of YHWH have become opponents of YHWH's intention. Thus the rich (5:5), the scribes (8:8), prophets and priests (8:10), the kings (shepherds) (9:21), the king and the royal family (10:18–19), and the nobles are all indicted for pursuing policies and actions that contradict the will of YHWH.

The most important critical assaults of rhetoric are reserved for two modes of leadership: prophets and kings. We have already considered the savage critique of "false prophets" in 23:6–22. That polemic is no doubt more acute because the "good news messengers" were the very ones who gave theological legitimacy to the royal policies that would bring destruction (see Ezek 13). But in the end it is not the prophets but the kings who are answerable for destructive policies. The kings are indicted for their policies that will bring devastation on the public realm. In Jeremiah 23:1–2, the "shepherds" (that is, the kings) are indicted (in a passage parallel to Ezek 34) and are said to be culpable for the "scattering" (exile) of the people.

A more extravagant indictment of kings is found in Jeremiah 22:13–19. Although the poetry does not specify which king is the subject of the oracle, the prose notation in verse 18 makes clear that the prophetic polemic is against Jehoiakim (see 2 Kings 23:34–24:7). This latter prose indictment suggests that it was resistance to Nebuchadnezzar that evoked divine judgment. This is a view that dominates the later traditions of the Book of Jeremiah. In Jeremiah 22, however, in poetic understatement, the indictment concerns not bad foreign policy but economic policy that features a royal rapacious acquisitiveness:

> But your eyes and heart
> are only on your dishonest gain,
> for shedding innocent blood,
> and for practicing oppression and violence. (Jer 22:17)

That policy, in contrast to that of his father Josiah (see Jer 22:15–16), will bring Jehoiakim to a shameful demise:

> With the burial of a donkey he shall be buried –
> dragged off and thrown out beyond the gates of Jerusalem. (Jer 22:19)

This review of the data makes clear that the poetic rhetoric of Jeremiah is rich, diverse, and complex in its articulation of divine judgment coming on Jerusalem. The substance of that judgment is simple to articulate. The prophetic tradition, however, is at pains to offer a rhetorical access to it so that the listening/reading community can enter into the loss from a variety of angles. The language of divine judgment that anticipates suffering, exile, and death is performative. *Thus the text itself becomes an arena of divine judgment through which listening Israel faces its fate.* The rhetoric is open, teasing, and elusive, for it means to draw Israel into the very presence of divine anger, divine pathos, and divine helplessness. For that reason, the rhetoric is quite varied, portraying YHWH as agent, as guarantor, and as passive observer. The loss of (and for) city and people is unutterable because it is the very mystery of God that causes the end. The theology of the Book of Jeremiah is an exercise in uttering what cannot be uttered.[42]

Judgment in the Prose Tradition

While the poetic tradition of divine judgment remains deliberately and artistically elusive, the prose tradition of the book draws us much closer to the Realpolitik of the seventh–sixth centuries BCE. The explicitly Deuteronomic formulation of chapters 7 and 18 present a radical either/or of Torah obedience. In the famous "Temple Sermon" of chapter 7, the prophet issues a series of requirements that are conditions for remaining in the land of promise:

> For if you truly amend your ways and your doings, if you truly act justly one with another, if you do not oppress the alien, the orphan, and the widow, or shed innocent blood in this place, and if you do not go after other gods to your own hurt, then I will dwell with you in this place, in the land that I gave of old to your ancestors forever and ever. (Jer 7:5–7)

While the opening verses of the chapter leave available a possibility of land retention, the latter part of the chapter moves on, no doubt in derivative rhetoric, to foreclose the option of the future and to declare divine wrath that will come on the city. The prophet is commanded not to intercede any longer for the city (v. 16; see also 11:14). The indictment of verses 23–28 is that Israel did not "listen"; that is, obey. The consequence is death (vv. 32–33) and a cessation of public life (v. 34).

---

[42] The actual practice of the canonical Book of Jeremiah is an instance of the aphorism of Barth in *The Word of God and the Word of Man*, 186: "As ministers we ought to speak of God. We are human, however, and so cannot speak of God. We ought therefore to recognize both our obligation and our inability and by that very recognition give God the glory. That is our perplexity."

In parallel fashion, 18:1–11 presents a symmetrical "either/or" that makes a bid in verse 11 to return to Torah obedience. That offer, however, is trumped in verse 12 in a closure indicating that the disobedience of Israel is beyond reversal. The certitude of judgment is unexpressed but also unmistakable:

> But they say, "It is no use! We will follow our own plans, and each of us will act according to the stubbornness of our evil will." (Jer 18:12)

Autonomous plans, whether for acquisitive economic policy or foolhardy military policy, can only end in destructiveness. The certainty about coming judgment is obvious in the enacted parable of the loincloth that is buried and then dug up and found "ruined . . . good for nothing" (13:7). Like the loincloth, Jerusalem will be "good for nothing" (v. 10). It is Yhwh's long-term intention that Israel will "cling" (*dbq*) to Yhwh as a loincloth clings to one's body. (See the same verb in Deut 13:4.)

But Israel would not listen (v. 11)! "Not listening" is a hopeless effort at autonomy, the ultimate affront to Yhwh, an affront that brings certain judgment. The same conclusion is drawn in 19:1–11; here the image is a potter – Israel as clay and Yhwh as potter (see 18:6; cf. Isa 45:9; 64:8). The pot displeases the potter . . . and so is smashed . . . beyond retrieval or reconstruction (Jer 19:11). These harsh verdicts in 13:10 and 19:11 still remain somewhat figurative. It is not until 20:4–6 that the prose tradition of Jeremiah finally draws the reader to the explicit geopolitical crisis of sixth-century BCE Jerusalem, "namely" the imperial threat of expansionist Babylon.

Here, for the first time, the Book of Jeremiah makes explicit that it is Babylon that will be the agent of Jerusalem's destruction. From this point on, Babylon dominates the rhetoric of the book. But John Hill has recently argued that Babylon is also the organizing principle, even if unnamed, of all of chapters 2–20:

The analysis of the figure of Babylon in chaps. 2–20 consisted of two phases. The first was the study of 20:1–6, the first text in the book which mentions Babylon explicitly. Within these verses Babylon was identified as a metaphor for being landless, and as such represented the reversal of the patriarchal traditions about the gift of the land. As a place it represents death for the exiles. In the future of its king it was presented as the one who invades, captures, exiles, kills and plunders Judah and its people.

The second phase of the analysis was a study of Babylon as an organising metaphor within chaps. 2–20. The figure of Babylon in these chapters is that of a metaphor around which the network of metaphors associated with Yhwh's judgment is organised. In particular, it subsumes the metaphors for invasion, banishment and death by the sword. The foundation of such an understanding of Babylon is the links between 20:1–6 and previous passages in chaps. 2–20 about Yhwh's judgment on Judah.

Because of the position of 20:1–6 within chaps. 2–20, the figure of Babylon as a metaphor points both backwards and forwards. In its function as an organising metaphor, it points backwards. After reading 20:1–6 the reader is sent back to the individual metaphors of judgment and can interpret them in the light of Babylon's function as an organising metaphor. In these chapters there are threats of the invasion and captivity of Judah, but the invader or captor is never identified. There are threats of banishment, but neither the agent nor the place of banishment are identified. There are also references to death and destruction, but the destroyers and plunderers are not identified. Then in 20:1–6, near the end of chaps. 2–20, the figure of Babylon appears, drawing together and representing the disparate metaphors for judgment which are otherwise unorganised and often unrelated. As an organising metaphor the figure of Babylon gives a focus to the material in chaps. 2–20.[43]

Whatever the case, most important for our purposes is the core claim of the prose tradition that Babylon is a tool of Yhwh in

---

[43] Hill, *Friend or Foe?* 71–72.

the coming destruction of Jerusalem and, as such, does not act unilaterally:

> For thus says the LORD: I am making you a terror to yourself and to all your friends; and they shall fall by the sword of their enemies while you look on. And I will give all Judah into the hand of the king of Babylon; he shall carry them captive to Babylon, and shall kill them with the sword. I will give all the wealth of this city, all its gains, all its prized belongings, and all the treasures of the kings of Judah into the hand of their enemies, who shall plunder them, and seize them, and carry them to Babylon. (Jer 20:4–5)

Although Babylon is of immense importance geopolitically, when understood theologically, Babylon is a mere function of YHWH's sovereignty. Babylon becomes a necessary strategy and device for YHWH's governance. Nebuchadnezzar, king of Babylon, moreover, is "my servant," who will enact YHWH's intent whereby all of the land is brought, albeit unwillingly, to YHWH's purpose (25:9; 27:6).

The prose material of judgment thus becomes a reflection on the way in which YHWH – through Babylon – executes harsh sovereignty over Jerusalem. In 21:1–2, Zedekiah, Jerusalem's final king (see 2 Kings 24:18–25:7), begs Jeremiah to petition YHWH for a miracle. Schooled in Israel's liturgy that celebrates YHWH's "mighty deeds," Zedekiah asks for one more such miracle, this time the deliverance of Jerusalem from the Babylonian threat. This royal request to the prophet in itself serves to narrate both the deconstruction of failed royal authority and the commensurate elevation of prophetic authority in the person of Jeremiah. The prophet responds to the king with an unwelcome assurance that there will indeed be a "divine wonder." That wonder, however, is not what the king anticipated or requested. It will be, instead, a massive unleashing of Babylonian military power against Jerusalem. The army belongs to Nebuchadnezzar, but the intent belongs to Y<small>HWH</small>, who has now declared war against Jerusalem:

> I myself will fight against you with outstretched hand and mighty arm, in anger, in fury, and in great wrath. (Jer 21:5)[44]

The divine wrath will not quit until there is a total exhaustion of pity and compassion:

> He shall strike them down with the edge of the sword; he shall not pity them, or spare them, or have compassion. (Jer 21:7b)

Nebuchadnezzar will not have pity on Jerusalem because Y<small>HWH</small> is not in the mood for pity.[45]

A parallel encounter between king and prophet is narrated in chapters 37–38, to the effect that the king is helpless and the prophet, under divine guidance, is completely committed to Babylon as a tool of Y<small>HWH</small>'s wrath. In 37:3, the king again petitions the prophet, and again the prophetic response is one of complete rejection (37:8–10). And, again, in 37:17, the king petitions and the prophet responds. Finally, in 38:17–23, this theology of Babylonian judgment is stated in symmetrical, perhaps Deuteronomic, phrasing. The positive "if" of the surrender to Babylon (which is the divine intent) will yield the positive "then" of the safety of life and city (v. 17). The negative "if" of resistance to Babylon (v. 18) will lead to a "then" of massive destruction, fire, and deportation (v. 18). It is clear that, by this time in the developing prophetic tradition, the prophetic imagination about divine judgment has

---

[44]See Moran, "The End of the Unholy War," 333–42.

[45] See Walter Brueggemann, "At the Mercy of Babylon: A Subversive Rereading of the Empire," *JBL* 110 (1991): 3–22, reprinted in *A Social Reading of the Old Testament: Prophetic Approaches to Israel's Communal Life*, ed. Patrick D. Miller (Minneapolis: Fortress, 1994), 111–33.

become quite centered and specific about the facts on the ground. For the developing tradition, the irresistible power of Babylon is a defining fact on the ground. And that fact is understood as YHWH's intention for Jerusalem. It is YHWH's will that Jerusalem should submit to Nebuchadnezzar. One may note that this judgment is also a highly pragmatic one: better to surrender than to have the city sacked.[46]

But the pragmatic argument is not the one made here. The hard truth of this tradition is that YHWH wills the city devastated and has evoked Babylon to do that task. All that can be seen by the normal observers is the Realpolitik of Babylonian imperial expansion. The prophet who has stood in the divine council, however, knows better. This is not merely military adventurism on the part of Babylon. This is *divine purpose*, the purpose of punishing Israel in its disobedience. Judgment is real, concrete, devastating, and irreversible. What it certainly is not, however, is "supernatural." Rather, it takes place *through visible, historical agents and affairs*. Once again, we see the prophetic imagination at work interpreting and connecting, with the result that *theological claim* and *lived public reality* are seen to be coherent.

Jeremiah and God's Sovereign Judgment

In the event of 587 BCE, of course, the connection made by the prophet is said to be vindicated. There is no thought of Babylonian autonomy or adventurism. In the tradition of Jeremiah, the judgment is all about divine sovereignty. This judgment is the work of the incomparable God who will not be mocked. Israel, Judah, and Jerusalem in their history of autonomy pursued

---

[46]This same strategy saved the city of Savannah, Georgia, from the ravages of General Sherman during the U.S. Civil War.

policies – economic and military – that violated the divine purpose. The claim of the Jeremian tradition is that, sooner or later, public history – governed by Y<small>HWH</small> in hidden ways – will circle around to reject such fantasy. The judgment is not only harsh in what is experienced but also unbearably demanding as an interpretive act. Jeremiah the man and the book voice the theological judgment about historical reality. It is no wonder that the one who voices such judgment lives in deep dispute with and protests against the God whose judgment must be proclaimed.

It is clear that the articulation of divine judgment requires a concrete adjudication of visible reality. Judgment here is specific and not generic. The voice of Jeremiah had to take sides on important policy questions. It is for that reason that Jeremiah is accused in the prose narrative as a deserter (37:13) and a traitor (38:4). Submission to Babylon was seen to "undermine the war effort." Thus the judgment of Y<small>HWH</small> placed the human spokesperson in an acutely unpopular position. At the same time, we know from the "Lamentations of Jeremiah" that he himself resisted such a vocation and felt exposed to danger and abandoned by the God who had sent him.[47] It is difficult enough to entertain the pro-Babylonian policy of the God of Israel. It is even more difficult to imagine the human vehicle of such a policy and the costs of such articulation. As always in the tradition of Jeremiah, the messenger is not readily distanced from the message. The pro-Babylonian words may be the "words of Jeremiah." But he is the one "to whom the word of the L<small>ORD</small> came." Everything turns on the utterance of hard words that grow out of the word of the L<small>ORD</small>.

---

[47] On the Lamentations of Jeremiah, see O'Connor, *The Confessions of Jeremiah*; Diamond, *The Confessions of Jeremiah in Context*; and Smith, *The Laments of Jeremiah and Their Contexts*.

The victory of Babylon over Jerusalem is complete. The prophetic tradition is vindicated. That victory is narrated in 39:1–10 (see 2 Kings 25:8–12). The recalcitrant covenant partner Israel is reduced to a sorry vassal state. Jeremiah 40–41 reports the "Babylonian peace" imposed on Judah through a Judean governor, Gedeliah, a son of the pro-Babylonian party in Jerusalem. It is clear that this governorship was unstable from the outset and not sustainable.

What may interest us most in this context is the awareness of the person of Jeremiah by the Babylonians:

> Take him, look after him well and do him no harm, but deal with him as he may ask you. (Jer 39:12)

> The captain of the guard took Jeremiah and said to him, "The LORD your God threatened this place with this disaster; and now the LORD has brought it about, and has done as he said, because all of you sinned against the LORD and did not obey his voice. Therefore this thing has come upon you. Now look, I have just released you today from the fetters on your hands. If you wish to come with me to Babylon, come, and I will take good care of you; but if you do not wish to come with me to Babylon, you need not come. See, the whole land is before you; go wherever you think it good and right to go. If you remain, then return to Gedaliah son of Ahikam son of Shaphan, whom the king of Babylon appointed governor of the towns of Judah, and stay with him among the people; or go wherever you think it right to go." So the captain of the guard gave him an allowance of food and a present, and let him go. Then Jeremiah went to Gedaliah son of Ahikam at Mizpah, and stayed with him among the people who were left in the land. (Jer 40:2–6)

Jeremiah is publicly recognized as a proponent of the Babylonian conquest. This recognition was no doubt at a political level, without any interest in theological claims or motivations. What is quite interesting, however, is that the tradition of Jeremiah features the prophet in this way and is completely unembarrassed that the prophet is readily allied with the enemy who accommodates him. This can only be taken as an indication of how deeply the ongoing Jeremian tradition was convinced of the truth of their pro-Babylonian position. Such a conviction could not fail to be informed by the Babylonian facts on the ground.

In any case, Jeremiah became, in this moment of vindication, a vehicle for the emerging authority of Babylonian Judaism in its dispute with the Jews who remained in Jerusalem and, particularly, in sharp dispute with the Jews in Egypt who competed with the Babylonian claims (see Jer 42–44). The vindication of the prophetic announcement of judgment makes the pro-Babylonian perspective of the Jeremian tradition so dominant that it will eventually prevail through the work of Ezra. The triumph of one interpretive community of Jews over another in a highly contested interpretive matter makes it clear that the exercise of prophetic leadership that connects *divine purpose* and *lived reality* is a daring, high-risk vocation. Such prophetic risk – so evident in the Book of Jeremiah – *requires taking sides about concrete questions before all of the data are in.* Jeremiah and his interpretive community had, it is asserted, rightly discerned the shape of Yнwн's governance into the future. That shape was definingly Babylonian. The rightness of that assertion well positioned the Jeremian tradition for a future in emerging Judaism.

Babylonian Domination: Complete and Penultimate

Although the poetry of Jeremiah is quite vivid and concrete, it is in fact elusive about the actual character of divine judgment. The prose, however, becomes quite explicit concerning Babylon as the agent of Yнwн's wrath. We may notice in particular the reference to Babylon in chapter 37.[48] In verses 5–6, Nebuchadnezzar is a

---

[48] See Hill, *Friend or Foe?* 129–44.

function of divine sovereignty. As Hill has noticed, the operative word is "serve" (*'bd*):

> All the nations shall *serve* [*wĕʿābĕdû*] him and his son and his grandson. (Jer 27:7)

> But if any nation or kingdom will not *serve* [*lōʾ-yaʿabdû*] this king, Nebuchadnezzar of Babylon, and put its neck under the yoke of the king of Babylon, then I will punish that nation with the sword, with famine, and with pestilence, says the LORD, until I have completed its destruction by his hand. (Jer 27:8)

> I spoke to King Zedekiah of Judah in the same way: Bring your necks under the yoke of the king of Babylon, and *serve* [*wĕʿibdû*] him and his people, and live. (Jer 27:12)

The judgment of YHWH in the form of Babylonian aggression will be total. And here the account of divine judgment ends. The turn of events in Jerusalem matches the prophetic anticipation. Jerusalem is indeed razed, the king is deported, the state is terminated, and the temple vessels are confiscated (2 Kings 25:1–21; Jer 39:1–10).[49]

In chapter 27, however, we may notice a repeated rhetorical maneuver that makes the judgment of Jerusalem – spoken and then enacted – *penultimate*. In this chapter, the adverb "until" (*'ad*) is used three times in a way that makes the divine judgment of Jerusalem less than ultimate:

> All the nations shall serve him and his son and his grandson, *until* [*'ad*] the time of his own land comes; then many nations and great kings shall make him their slave. (Jer 27:7; see also v. 8)

> They shall be carried to Babylon, and there they shall stay, *until* [*'ad*] the day when I give attention to them, says the LORD. Then I will bring them up and restore them to this place. (Jer 27:22)

---

[49] On the symbolic significance of the temple vessels in the drama of deportation and restoration, see Peter R. Ackroyd, "The Temple Vessels: A Continuity Theme," in his *Studies in the Religious Tradition of the Old Testament* (London: SCM, 1987), 46–60.

By this maneuver, the Jeremian tradition limits the punishment of Jerusalem, reverses field, and begins to anticipate the ultimate divine judgment on Babylon. Thus the judgment of Jerusalem is displaced and overridden in this rhetoric by divine judgment on the great empire that had imagined itself (in its recalcitrant ignorance) to be autonomous and accountable to no one. Understood historically, we may assume that this decisive addendum looks to the collapse of Babylon in the coming victory of Cyrus the Persian over Babylon.

If, however, we consider the matter theologically, it becomes clear that Yhwh's massive sovereignty is always only provisionally allied with any earthly power. Thus, in 27:5–6, there is no doubt that divine sovereignty is committed to the success of Babylon. In verse 7, however, that divine commitment is for the short term; in the end, Yhwh's sovereignty concerns only Yhwh's rule and Yhwh's glory, and no earthly power dare imagine it will finally share in the divine splendor. The "until" of 27:7 anticipates that, by divine decrees, Babylon will be reduced to servitude. The "until" of verse 22 likewise anticipates that Yhwh will reverse fields and "give attention" to the Jews in Babylon. In verse 8, the "until" indicates that Babylon's task is only to complete the destruction of Jerusalem. After that, Yhwh has no more business to conduct through Babylon, who is subsequently of no further use. In 29:10, the "until" of chapter 27 is reduced to a standard formula of "seventy years," but that formulation only serves to specify the terms of "until."

Yhwh's Sovereignty Unbounded

So it is that the Book of Jeremiah culminates in an anticipation that Yhwh will destroy the ultimate superpower of the time; that destruction, moreover, will be an opening for the restoration and future well-being of Jerusalem. This sequence of judgment from

Jerusalem to Babylon reminds one that Jeremiah's call is to be a prophet "to the nations" (1:5, 10). The Book of Jeremiah thus finishes in very large scope, witnessing to the global governance of YHWH, which in the end is completely to the advantage of Jerusalem and Israel, "the portion of Jacob . . . the tribe of his inheritance" (10:16). The culmination of the book thus is a celebration of YHWH's full sovereignty, a rule that holds positive promise for the city of Jerusalem, which has been severely judged. Two texts in particular move the Jeremian tradition toward this large, positive conclusion.

First, chapter 25 shows the sequence of judgments that are traced in the book.[50] Verses 1–8 indict Judah for not listening. Verse 8 introduces a great "therefore" of judgment, a declaration that extends through verse 11. In verses 8–11, the Babylonians are to be unleashed against the city. But "then," after seventy years, the field is reversed and it is Babylon that will be punished and devastated (v. 12). Verses 12–13 thus reflect a belated stage in the sequence of divine judgment. From these lead verses, we note the tradition developing in two directions. In 25:14, Babylon is reduced to servitude ('*bd*). But then in verse 15 the text moves in a quite different direction, anticipating radical and savage divine judgment on "all the nations." The constant reference of verses 19–26 is about "all the kingdoms," which are now to be brought, even in resistance, under the rule of YHWH:

---

[50] Chapter 25, which stands at the center of the canonical form of the Book of Jeremiah, is quite exceptional in the book and likely performs a peculiar and important function for the whole of the book. See Martin Kessler, "The Function of Chapters 25 and 50–51 in the Book of Jeremiah," in *Troubling Jeremiah*, ed. A. R. Pete Diamond, Kathleen M. O'Connor, and Louis Stulman, JSOTSup 260 (Sheffield: Sheffield Academic Press, 1999), 64–72; and John Hill, "The Construction of Time in Jeremiah 25 MT," in *Troubling Jeremiah*, ed. Diamond et al., 146–60.

See, I am beginning to bring disaster on the city that is called by my name, and how can you possibly avoid punishment? You shall not go unpunished, for I am summoning a sword against all the inhabitants of the earth, says the LORD of hosts. (Jer 25:29)

> The clamor will resound to the ends of the earth,
> for the LORD has an indictment against the nations;
> he is entering into judgment with all flesh,
> and the guilty he will put to the sword,
> says the LORD. (Jer 25:31–32)

The focus is no longer on Israel or Jerusalem alone; the apocalyptic tenor of these verses concerns wholesale, global judgment in the interest of asserting YHWH's rule. In this text, YHWH has no allies and surely "takes no prisoners." This sovereignty is manifested as wholesale devastation.

Two references in 25:13 to "everything written in the book which Jeremiah prophesied against the nations" evokes the *second* text – better, texts – that demonstrate YHWH's full sovereignty. In the LXX, the Oracles Against the Nations in Jeremiah 46–51 are placed just after verse 13. The connection between chapter 25 and chapters 46–51 is another indication of how the tradition articulates YHWH's rule over the nations and Jeremiah's vocation as a "prophet to the nations."

The corpus of Oracles Against the Nations in chapters 46–51 concerns the way in which every nation is, in the end, subject to YHWH's unaccommodating rule. Yet, even in that corpus, it seems to be the case that while many nations are listed in a stylized way, the focus of interest is ultimately Babylon in chapters 50–51.[51] The

---

[51] On this text, see Martin Kessler, *Battle of the Gods: The God of Israel Versus Marduk of Babylon – A Literary/Theological Interpretation of Jeremiah 50–51*, SSN 42 (Assen: Van Gorcum, 2003).

tenor of divine judgment in chapters 25 and 46–51 anticipates the
later lyrical Christian affirmation of Revelation 11:15:

> The kingdom of the world has
> become the kingdom of our LORD
> and of his Messiah,
> and he will reign forever and ever. (Rev 11:15)

In the specific case of Jeremiah 50–51 concerning Babylon, the
premise of the whole is Babylon's defeat:

> Declare among the nations and proclaim,
> set up a banner and proclaim,
> do not conceal it, say:
> *Babylon is taken,*
> Bel is put to shame,
> Merodach is dismayed.
> Her images are put to shame,
> her idols are dismayed. (Jer 50:2)

The kingdom used by YHWH is now judged in its arrogance and
found wanting (see 50:31–32).[52] We may identify four aspects of
this text for consideration, though the poem itself is complex and
rich with interpretive possibilities.

First, YHWH wills the destruction of Babylon and will effect its
devastation by an unnamed invader. The key verb with YHWH as
subject is *'wr*, "stir up." YHWH, as ruler of all nations, will arouse
a new agent who will move against Babylon. YHWH's alliance with
Babylon is now terminated:

> For I am going to *stir up* [*mēʿîr*] and bring against Babylon a company
> of great nations from the land of the north; and they shall array
> themselves against her; from there she shall be taken. Their arrows

---

[52] On imperial hybris, see Donald E. Gowan, *When Man Becomes God: Humanism
and Hybris in the Old Testament*, PTMS 6 (Pittsburgh, PA: Pickwick, 1975).

are like the arrows of a skilled warrior who does not return empty-handed. Chaldea shall be plundered; all who plunder her shall be sated, says the LORD. (Jer 50:9–10)

> Thus says the LORD:
> I am going to *stir up* [*mē'îr*] a destructive wind against Babylon
> and against the inhabitants of Lebqamai;
> and I will send winnowers to Babylon,
> and they shall winnow her.
> They shall empty her land
> when they come against her from every side
> on the day of trouble. (Jer 51:1–2; see Isa 41:2)

The verb *'wr* wondrously testifies to YHWH's hidden, elusive rule of the public process. The "stirred up" entity is here left unspecified, but in 2 Chronicles 36:22, a citation of Jeremiah is offered, replete with concrete identification of Cyrus the Persian as the one mobilized by YHWH to defeat Babylon (see also Isa 44:28; 45:1).

Second, this poetry concerning Babylon recycles material we have already considered, indicating that the *judgment against Babylon* is an important echo and counterpoint of the *judgment against Jerusalem*. Thus Jeremiah 6:22–23, a poetic unit anticipating the invasion of Judah, is now quoted, this time concerning a threat *against Babylon*:

> Look, a people is coming from the north;
> a mighty nation and many kings
> are stirring [*yē'ōrû*] from the farthest parts of the earth.
> They wield bow and spear,
> they are cruel and have no mercy.
> The sound of them is like the roaring sea;
> they ride upon horses,
> set in array as a warrior for battle,
> against you, O daughter Babylon! (Jer 50:41–42)

In both of these cases, the same verb, "stir" (*'wr*), is used. Just as Nebuchadnezzar showed "no mercy," so now Babylon will receive "no mercy" from Cyrus (see Isaiah 47).

Third, in 51:15–19, parts of the poem in 10:1–16 are recycled; in chapter 10, the assault on the idols was rather generic, asserting the incomparability of YHWH the creator God. When the poetry is placed in the oracle against Babylon, however, the same accents take on new force. In this latter context, the singularity of YHWH is juxtaposed with Babylonian pretensions and Babylonian gods. The praise of YHWH in this text, as in 10:1–16, is perhaps to be understood according to the self-praise of YHWH in 27:5: "It is I." Only in chapter 51 is it "It is he." The "I" of YHWH or the "he" of YHWH is beyond challenge and will tolerate no imperial pretension. As the idols are generically dismissed in 10:1–16, in 51:15–19 it is the pretense of Babylon that is dismissed.

Fourth, the rhetoric of this text concerns the destruction of Babylon. Quite clearly, the practical consequence of that destruction is a new chance for Jews in exile to return to Jerusalem. Thus, the second wave of judgment serves finally to move beyond the first wave of judgment of Babylon and to create ground for a new possibility. This is evident in a number of places in the oracle against Babylon wherein YHWH finally will not fail Jerusalem:

> I will restore Israel to its pasture, and it shall feed on Carmel and in Bashan, and on the hills of Ephraim and in Gilead its hunger shall be satisfied. In those days and at that time, says the LORD, the iniquity of Israel shall be sought, and there shall be none; and the sins of Judah, and none shall be found; for I will pardon the remnant that I have spared. (Jer 50:19–20; see also vv. 4–5, 28)

> Come out of her, my people!
> Save your lives, each of you,
> from the fierce anger of the LORD!

> Do not be fainthearted or fearful
> at the rumors heard in the land –
> one year one rumor comes,
> the next year another,
> rumors of violence in the land
> and of ruler against ruler. (Jer
> 51:45–46; see also vv. 36–37)

There can be no doubt that the God of the Jeremian tradition is a severe sovereign whose sovereignty matches the turmoil and upheaval of geopolitics in the sixth century BCE. Through the utterance of the prophet, there has indeed been "plucking up and tearing down," first of Jerusalem and then of Babylon. But the prophet is not yet done. The prophet has a second mandate. It is to that second task that we now turn.

YHWH'S SOVEREIGNTY AS PROMISE

Jeremiah has been faithful to his prophetic vocation as "prophet to the nations" with the agenda that he must "pluck up and tear down" (1:10). This dismantling of Jerusalem and then of Babylon has been accomplished in poetic discourse by a rich complex of images, including the *rejection of infidelity*, the *invasion of war*, *terminal illness*, and *foolishness that leads to death*. All of these images serve as rhetorical strategies for divine judgment. The dismantling has been accomplished in the prose by evoking Babylon as the visible, irresistible agent of divine resolve. Through prose and poetry, the "end" has come upon Jerusalem, wrought by the rule of YHWH, who will not be mocked.

At this point, the matter of Jerusalem and the Book of Jeremiah might have rested, except that in historical circumstances, life goes on; except that the rule of YHWH continues to be generative; and except that Jeremiah's prophetic vocation included a mandate to "plant and build" – a mandate enacted in performative speech that is promise-laden. There can be no doubt that the tradition of Jeremiah fully embraces and enacts "plucking up and tearing down." With equal force, however, the ongoing tradition of Jeremiah makes clear that YHWH's purpose for Jerusalem, after destruction, is indeed restoration. Thus, two pairs of verbs in the prophetic call of 1:10 are programmatically sequenced in 31:28:

> And just as I have watched over them to pluck up and break down, to overthrow, destroy, and bring evil, so I will watch over them *to build* and *to plant*, says the LORD. (Jer 31:28)

The God who "watched over my work to perform it" (1:12), concerning destruction, is the God who will now watch to see that the work of "plant and build" is fully enacted. The move from one accent to the other, taken theologically, can only be grounded in YHWH's firm resolve not only to rule but to rule *from Jerusalem, in and through Israel.* Although the Book of Jeremiah is not neatly ordered, as we have now seen, in general the second half of the book (from chapter 24 on) offers a variety of strategies for restoration.

There was indeed a deep ending for Jerusalem. But as quickly as that ending is articulated, so quickly does the voice of Jeremiah affirm that the end is not finally an end:[53]

> For thus says the LORD: The whole land shall be a desolation; yet I will *not make a full end.* (Jer 4:27)

> > Go up through her vine-rows and destroy,
> > but do *not make a full end;*

---

[53] See Walter Brueggemann, "An Ending that Does Not End: The Book of Jeremiah," in *Postmodern Interpretations of the Bible: A Reader*, ed. A. K. M. Adam (St. Louis, MO: Chalice, 2001), 117–28.

> strip away her branches,
> for they are not the LORD's. (Jer 5:10)

But even in those days, says the LORD, I will *not make a full end* of you. (Jer 5:18; see also 5:31)

> Alas! that day is so great
> there is none like it;
> it is a time of distress for Jacob;
> *yet he shall be rescued* from it. (Jer 30:7)

* * *

> But as for you, have no fear, my servant Jacob, says the LORD,
> and do not be dismayed, O Israel;
> for I am going to save you from far away,
> and your offspring from the land of their captivity.
> Jacob shall return and have quiet and ease,
> and no one shall make him afraid.
> For I am with you, says the LORD, to save you;
> I will make an end of all the nations
> among which I scattered you,
> but of you I will *not make an end.*
> I will chastise you in just measure,
> and I will by no means leave you unpunished. (Jer 30:10–11)

The wonder of YHWH's relation to Jerusalem is that judgment is penultimate. The ultimate word is rescue, deliverance, restoration, and homecoming, all grounded solely in divine resolve.

This making "the end" out to be penultimate after all is evident in the series of "untils" we have noted in 25:12–13 and 27:7, 8, 22, indicating that even the punishing power of Babylon, authorized by YHWH, is provisional. After a time of domination by the superpower Babylon, that superpower will go the way of all superpowers before the abiding resolve of YHWH, for "our little systems have their day, they have their day and cease to be." We have seen that the sorry history of Jerusalem turns on the deep indignation of YHWH. In the end, however, it is not *divine indignation* but *divine fidelity* to Israel that wins the day and that both causes and permits the Book of Jeremiah to move beyond "pluck up and tear down" to "plant and build." I will organize this discussion of "plant and build" around three groups of texts, with the second receiving primary attention.

Prose Beyond Destruction

We may begin with a scattering of prose texts that look beyond the destruction to the restoration of Jerusalem. These texts may reflect Deuteronomic influence because they tend to be conditioned on a return to Torah obedience. Thus they interpreted restoration as constituted by a full reentry of Israel into Torah obedience after a long season of foolish, death-inviting waywardness.

In 12:14 the verb "pluck up" is used twice but in a quite uncharacteristic fashion. Now "my people Israel" are to be "plucked up" from among "my evil neighbors"; that is, from the place in Babylon to which they had been deported. The verb "pluck up" is used a third time in verse 15, indicating that in compassion Yhwh will bring the deportees back to the land. In this text, as in so many in the tradition of Jeremiah, the future depends on the practice of the deportees, and the deportees came to constitute the future of Israel in the land. Thus verses 14–15 constitute a vow on the part of Yhwh for restoration. In verse 16, however, the initial compassion that makes homecoming possible is abruptly qualified by the "if" of Torah. Israel will return to the land. Its capacity to remain in the land, however, is not a free gift but depends on obedience. Without "listening" (*šmʿ*), that people will again be "plucked up" in wrath and destroyed (v. 17). This text anticipates a recovery of obedience to the covenant, the kind of obedience on which retention of land was already premised in Joshua 1:7, 16–18.

The second text is Jeremiah 29:10–14, in which the reference to "seventy years" reflects the "until" strategy already cited. Clearly, the residence in Babylon urged in 29:4–7 is limited. In due course, Yнwн will keep the promise of homecoming. Yнwн has a "plan" for the *shalom* of Israel (see Isa 55). The resolve of Yнwн is unambiguous. It is for *shalom* (v. 11). And *shalom* entails "gathering," which means an end of exilic scattering, the restoration of fortunes, and resettlement in the land. This statement is programmatic and includes most of the key phrasing that occurs in the hope of restoration. The whole is a declaration of Yнwн concerning the future.

It must be noted, however, that in verses 12–13 this unconditional declaration is premised on Israel's taking the initiative in calling to Yнwн. Israel is to seek for Yнwн with all its heart; that is, to return to the full obedience envisioned in Deuteronomy 6:4–5. The rhetoric of verse 13 would seem to be in the indicative mood – Yнwн has confidence in Israel's future behavior: "You will seek me." But the NRSV makes the statement conditional: "If you seek me." Either way, it is clear that Yнwн's promise for the future depends on Israel being deeply serious about a responsible relationship with Yнwн. This text has close affinity to Deuteronomy 4:29–31, also in the indicative; Deuteronomy 30:1–10; and 1 Kings 8, all of which summon Israel to repentance and come close to the rhetoric of conditionality.

A third prose text, Jeremiah 42:9–17, is clearly conditional. It offers a parallel of positive and negative "if-then" phrasing. Here the "if" that makes well-being possible is not a generic summons to Torah obedience but a particular decision to remain in the land of Israel; that is, to refuse to join the Jews in Egypt, who are here regarded as renegades. This text thus urges Jews to remain in a sphere of Babylonian influence, for at this point Jerusalem is

under Babylonian control. Such a decision yields an assurance that
Yhwh will grant mercy and that the king of Babylon will grant
mercy:

> Do not be afraid of the king of Babylon, as you have been; do not be
> afraid of him, says the Lord, for I am with you, to save you and to
> rescue you from his hand. I will grant you mercy, and he will have
> mercy on you and restore you to your native soil. (Jer 42:11–12)

It would seem plausible that this position of advocacy reflects those
who had allied themselves with the pro-Babylonian policy and who
in turn received favorable treatment from the occupying force, no
doubt a circle that revolved around Jeremiah and Shaphan. (The
negative counterpart in vv. 13–17 indicates the foolhardiness of
embracing the Egyptian option.) It is to be noted that in this text
there is no promise of homecoming because the text is addressed
to those for whom the only options are Jerusalem or Egypt. Thus
the pro-Babylonian constituency, surely led by the community in
Babylon, continued to lobby in Jerusalem because the future of
Jewishness was deeply contested. This text is exceedingly important
because it exhibits the way in which the theological conviction of
the tradition concerning the mercy of Yhwh is deeply connected
with the political–military facts on the ground.

"The Book of Comfort"

The second and most important group of promissory texts is found
in chapters 30–33, where the editorial process has clustered most of
the promises in the book. The primary promises of chapters 30–31
are referred to by scholars as "the Book of Comfort," an allusion to
30:2. The term "comfort" in such usage is informed by the famous
declaration of Isaiah 40:1, where "comfort" is news of permission
to go home. Attached to Jeremiah 30–31 is the narrative account of

chapter 32 concerning the future of the land and the addendum of promises in chapter 33.

Chapters 30–31, the principal cluster of promises in the Book of Jeremiah, include poems that are unqualified by any of the conditionality that we have seen in the prose pieces just cited. The sense of these two chapters is a massive assurance of YHWH's unilateral decision to enact a wondrous, joyous future for those who return to Jerusalem. These passages have much in common with the promises of Isaiah 40–55 and Ezekiel 33–37, which are also prophetic utterances that counter the lived reality of displacement. This entire complex of prophetic promises indicates an important sixth-century trajectory of hope, perhaps informed by the stirrings of Persia but for the most part grounded theologically in the conviction that YHWH is a future-generating God who will indeed "call into existence things that do not exist" (Rom 4:17).[54] What YHWH will now call into existence is a restored Israel in a restored city.

More specifically, we may note the rhetorical nuance of originary speech whereby the prophetic tradition gives concrete substance to the generative capacity of YHWH.

In Jeremiah 30:3, the initial prose promise in this unit utilizes the phrase "restore the fortunes" (*šûb šĕbût*). This phrase, a characteristic one in promissory declarations of the sixth-century BCE exile, asserts that YHWH, by an act of sovereign resolve, can abruptly reverse the situation of Israel in exile. In this case, the promise is

---

[54] The citation of Romans 4 is not inappropriate here because it appeals to the same Gospel in the sixth century BCE with particular reference to Abraham. By the time of the exile, it is clear that "Abraham" had become a cipher for promise. "Abraham" thus recurs in numerous exilic texts of promise; it is clear that Paul, in Romans, extends the force of the figure. The figure is ostensibly rooted in history but was then managed with enormous imagination in the tradition.

to turn exile into homecoming, to turn "scatter" into "gather," to turn death to life. To "restore the fortunes" looks to the inexplicable power of YHWH to create a newness; it does not refer to the facts on the ground whereby that newness may appear. That is as yet unclear.

The brief poetic unit in 30:10–11 constitutes a "salvation oracle," the utterance of the divine "fear not" that gives assurance of divine engagement and testifies to YHWH's resolve to override the current circumstance of trouble. These verses attest to YHWH's readiness to "save" – a term used twice here. Verse 11 assures that the onslaught by the Babylonians is for chastisement and not termination. The reference to "an end" of the nations that have "scattered" Israel is surely a typical anticipation in the Jeremian tradition culminating in chapters 50–51 concerning the defeat and destruction of Babylon. These verses speak powerfully against the apparent reality in which the "end" of Israel seemed at hand. That reality is countered by divine assurance that the suffering and displacement is only a temporary disruption, not a termination.

Jeremiah 30:12–17 is remarkable because it enacts, in poetic utterance, precisely the divine reversal promised in 30:3 and the rescue anticipated in 30:10–11.[55] Verses 12–15 reiterate the reality of the "sickness unto death" from chapter 8 and justify that dismal future for Israel on the basis of its great guilt. Thus verses 12–15 by themselves are not at all promissory. They function, however, to underscore the rhetorical surprise created by verses 16–17, which is introduced by an ominous "therefore." In these latter verses, the

---

[55] On this text, see Walter Brueggemann, "The 'Uncared For' Now Cared For (Jeremiah 30:12–17): A Methodological Consideration," *JBL* 104 (1985): 419–28, reprinted in *Old Testament Theology: Essays on Structure, Theme, and Text*, ed. Patrick D. Miller (Minneapolis: Fortress, 1992), 296–307.

threat of sickness to death is radically countered, so that the God resigned to the death of Israel in 8:18–22 now promises a complete recovery:

> For I will restore health to you,
> and your wounds I will heal, says the LORD,
> because they have called you an outcast:
> "It is Zion; no one cares for her!" (Jer 30:17)

The grounds for the healing in verse 17 is that YHWH will not permit the nations to mock Zion, even though that mocking in verse 17 by the nations does little else but echo YHWH's own words in verse 14. Thus, the two parts of this unit, verses 12–15 and verses 16–17, enact judgment and restoration, deportation and homecoming, or – to use the primal phrasing of Jeremiah – "plucking up and tearing down . . . building and planting." The leap from verse 15 to verse 16 is the leap of divine newness that is only possible in YHWH's fresh resolve that the poem brings to speech.

Jeremiah 30:18–22 begins with a reiteration of the tag phrase "restore the fortunes" and culminates in verse 22 with a standard "covenant formula" that recurs in exile to indicate the abiding quality of the YHWH–Israel relationship.[56] The material between the phrases in verse 18 and verse 22 bespeaks the concrete sociopolitical restoration of the city under the verb "build" (v. 18). Verses 19–20 anticipate the resumption of social life and, remarkably, verse 21 anticipates a restored "ruler," perhaps a king. Verse 24 plays on the "until" that was discussed earlier; the usage indicates both long-term suffering and the fact that this suffering is limited. The last lines of the verse indicate a late apocalyptic development when only

---

[56] On the covenant formula, see Rolf Rendtorff, *Covenant Formula: An Exegetical and Theological Investigation* (Edinburgh: T. and T. Clark, 1998); and Rudolf Smend, *Die Bundesformel*, ThSt 68 (Zürich: EVZ-Verlag, 1963).

the initiated, later on, will understand the great drama of death and new life.

The beginning verses of chapter 31 offer wondrous phrasings of hope. In verse 1, the covenant formula is reiterated. In verse 2, it is promised that there is "grace in the wilderness." The two terms "grace" and "wilderness" are intrinsically antithetical to each other. The term "wilderness" here refers to the exile and is typically a place without divine presence or favor. The point of the poetry, however, is precisely to contradict the assumption that exile is devoid of YHWH's care and protection. Thus the tradition here champions the exile as the matrix of the future community that YHWH will generate. In such a claim, the phrasing surely appeals to Hosea 2:14–25, where divine love is articulated in the wilderness; it perhaps also alludes to the narrative of Exodus 16–17, wherein Israel attests to divine sustenance in the wilderness. The great prophetic promises of Isaiah, Jeremiah, and Ezekiel all attest, against common assumption, that divine goodness is offered exactly to exiles, a point greatly affirmed in Jeremiah 24:

> I will set my eyes upon them for good, and I will bring them back to this land. I will build them up, and not tear them down; I will plant them, and not pluck them up. I will give them a heart to know that I am the LORD; and they shall be my people and I will be their God, for they shall return to me with their whole heart. (Jer 24:6–7)

In Jeremiah 31:3, the sentiment of verse 2 is reinforced by the astonishing assurance, "I have loved you with an abiding love." This statement asserts that even the displacement of exile did not signify divine rejection; rather, YHWH has been caring for, doting on, and being faithful to Israel throughout the displacement.

After the rich relational vocabulary of verses 1–3, verses 4–6 return to the rhetoric of political restoration. The future is not just

a good relationship but includes a restored urban political infra-
structure signified by the paradigmatic verbs "build and plant." A
genuine resumption of communal life is anticipated!

It should be noted in verse 7 that the restoration concerns a
"remnant." The hope for Israel's future is realistic and anticipates
a small community "gathered" from Babylon (v. 8). More will be
said about the remnant.

The "two-stage theology" of the Jeremian tradition, fully
reflected in the verbs of 1:10, is voiced succinctly in 31:10:

> Hear the word of the LORD, O nations,
> and declare it in the coastlands far away;
> say, "He who *scattered* Israel will *gather* him,
> and will keep him as a shepherd a flock." (Jer 31:10)

The God who caused exile ("scattered") is the God who will create
homecoming ("gather"). The scattering is not denied but is not
given final play because the culmination of the tradition, here so
vividly put, concerns restoration of urban life. The exile is, in the
end, penultimate, even though the early poetry is preoccupied with
it. Verse 11 employs the word for "ransom, redeem," language also
used in Isaiah 43 to signify that the restoration of Israel was indeed
"costly" to the God who brings Israel home.

Jeremiah 31:20 constitutes one of the most remarkable, pathos-
filled utterances in the Book of Jeremiah, or indeed in the entire
prophetic corpus.[57] The first two lines are rhetorical questions that
require an answer, "Yes." Yes, Ephraim is my dear son. Yes, he is
the child in whom I delight. The second pair of lines state YHWH's
dilemma, which is perhaps the clue to the entire tradition. On

---

[57] See the discussion of this text by Kazo Kitamori, *Theology of the Pain of God*
(Richmond, VA: John Knox, 1965).

the one hand, YHWH would like to speak against Ephraim, that
is, condemn and reject. On the other hand, when YHWH does so
speak, YHWH nonetheless remembers with compassion.[58] (The ver-
bal construction is emphatic: infinitive absolute + finite verb of
rḥm.) Israel is so much in YHWH's heart and mind that YHWH
is unable to forget, reject, speak against, or abandon it. For that
reason, YHWH's innards are disturbed and YHWH will have compassion. God *has compassion* because God *remembers*. But YHWH
remembers against YHWH's own propensity. YHWH has compassion against YHWH's will; YHWH cannot help but care. This savage
exposé of YHWH's internal struggle suggests that beneath the ire of
an offended sovereign is the care of a father (see v. 9), or, even better, the tender love of a mother who cannot in any case relinquish
the child. In this utterance, Israel's future is assured because YHWH
is internally and intensely unable to reject on account of YHWH's
love.[59]

The best-known promise in Jeremiah – at least in Christian interpretation – is Jeremiah 31:31–34 concerning the "new covenant."
Christian interpretation, with particular appeal to Hebrews 8:8–13,
has frequently read this text in the most vigorously supercessionist
way possible, as though the "new covenant" pertains only to the
Gospel of Jesus Christ, with Israel rejected for its broken covenant.
Of course, nothing could more distort the text than such a reading. The text is rather a divine declaration that YHWH will begin
again with Israel and restore a covenantal relationship that has been
lost in the debacle of disobedience and destruction. Two parts of

---

[58] On the compassion of YHWH, see James L. Kugel, *The God of Old: Inside the Lost World of the Bible* (New York: Simon and Schuster, 2004), 129–36.

[59] The primal study of YHWH's pathos is Heschel, *The Prophets*; see also Robinson, *The Cross in the Old Testament*.

the promise are of particular interest. First, *the shape of the new covenant relationship is according to the Torah*:

> But this is the covenant that I will make with the house of Israel after those days, says the LORD: I will put my law within them, and I will write it on their hearts; and I will be their God, and they shall be my people. (Jer 31:33)

The purpose of the new covenant, like the purpose of the old covenant, is to shape a people in obedience to the commands of Sinai. Given the tone of the Book of Jeremiah, it is likely that the "Torah" here in purview is the tradition of Deuteronomy. Second, *the grounds of the new covenant is divine forgiveness*:

> For I will forgive their iniquity, and remember their sin no more. (Jer 31:34b)

Unike elsewhere in the Book of Jeremiah, here there is no call for repentance. The newness is all on the side of YHWH's fresh inclination, the God who is incapable of not having a relationship with Israel. Thus the future for Israel depends on the sure resolve of YHWH to begin again, here even without preconditions.[60]

Whereas 31:31–34 concerns the immediacy of a renewed relationship after that relationship has been disrupted, the two fragments of 31:35–36 and 31:37 move in a very different direction (see also 33:19–22, 25). Here the appeal is not to covenantal fidelity but to

---

[60] The capacity of YHWH to begin again is evident in the flood narrative of Genesis 6:5–9:17. In both literary strands of the narrative, it is clear that nothing has changed about human practice or capacity through the course of the story. The change is in the propensity of YHWH to begin again. See also Jacqueline E. Lapsley, *Can These Bones Live? The Problem of the Moral Self in the Book of Ezekiel*, BZAW 301 (Berlin: de Gruyter, 2000), on the way in which the Ezekiel tradition moves from a summons to repent to the gift of newness from YHWH without precondition. See also Thomas M. Raitt, *A Theology of Exile: Judgment/Deliverance in Jeremiah and Ezekiel* (Philadelphia: Fortress, 1977).

the reliability of creation. These two statements assert that YHWH's commitment to Israel is as durable and trustworthy as is the very sustenance of creation. The inference to be drawn is that even the disruption of the sixth century BCE, so acute and central in the Book of Jeremiah, is in fact no final disruption after all, because YHWH's commitment to Israel is beyond disruption.

Finally, after this formidable affirmation of fidelity, which is said to be as sure as the cosmos, 31:38–40 become very specific about the reconstruction and restitution of Jerusalem. The final two verbs governed by "never again" are "uproot and overthrow," verbs that derive from 1:10. The "never again" that curbs any future disaster is the same "never again" as in the flood narrative (see Gen 8:22, 9:11, 15; and also Isa 54:9, where the imagery of the flood is linked to the sixth-century disaster).

The extraordinary richness of chapters 30–31 evidences the depth and complexity of the ways in which the Jeremian tradition can speak of this future-promising, future-creating God. The poetry of promise exploits the multiple traditions available from Israel's memory. All of that richness and complexity, however, serves a single purpose, "namely" the assurance that YHWH is faithful and powerful and intends a good new future for Israel's "welfare" – its *shalom* – a future with hope (see 29:11; 31:17).[61]

Four Themes of Hope
We can conclude by identifying four themes of hope that indicate some of the interests and voices that appear in Jeremiah.

[61] Chapters 32 and 33 are not commonly included in the primary promise material of "The Book of Comfort." Nonetheless, the narrative about land in chapter 32 and the series of promissory oracles in chapter 33 both attest to YHWH as a future-creating God.

First, there is no doubt that the displaced people in Babylon who present themselves as the carriers of Israel's identity into the future also present themselves as *a faithful remnant* preserved and loved by Yʜwʜ (see 31:7). Of particular importance in this regard is the formula "your life as a price of war," a phrase that refers to those who submit to Babylon (38:2) and particularly to Ebed-melech (39:18) and Baruch (45:5), two devoted to Jeremiah, who advocated Babylonian hegemony. The phrasing represents, in each case, a small subset of the community that, at some risk, allied itself with the policies advocated by Jeremiah. This particular remnant eventually offers itself, in the work of Ezra, as the "holy seed" for the time to come (Ezra 9:23; Neh 9:2). Thus, as the Jeremian tradition develops in new circumstances, we can see a transition to a remnant community with a hope commensurate with modest political ambitions and deep commitments to the Torah and the holiness traditions (see 23:3).

Second, it is curious that while the primal hopes of the Jeremian tradition are covenantal and are oriented toward the Torah, there is evidence of an energetic hope for *the restoration of the monarchy*. I have already cited 30:21. More formally, attention should be paid to 23:4 (wherein "shepherds" equals kings), 23:5–6, and 33:14–16. It is most likely that these monarchal scenarios are quite tangential to the primary trajectories of the Jeremian tradition. It is implausible that the Torah-oriented tradition should entertain a recovered monarchy, even as it declares the last king, Jehoiakin, to be without an heir (22:28–30). Nonetheless, these texts concerning Davidic futures indicate that hope for such royal restoration was so powerful that it could not be excluded from the final form of the text. In passing, we should also mention the culmination in 52:31–34, which may, in the end, entertain a royal possibility.

Third, alongside *remnant theology* and *royal theology*, notice should be taken of the climactic position of 36:32 and the scroll at the hand of Baruch, plus the scroll in 51:59–64 at the hand of Seraiah, brother of Baruch. If we provisionally delineate chapters 37–45 as a special narrative report and chapters 46–51 as Oracles Against the Nations, we may entertain the thought that 36:33 occupies something of a climactic position in the tradition. If that is so, then this possibility of *scribal production* – to be distinguished from both the remnant and the royal options – constitutes yet another mode of the future. This would suggest the conviction that Judaism in the time to come will amount to nothing more and nothing less than the normative scroll and an immense interpretive practice. Such a prospect for Judaism is suggested in the notation that the Ezra community was indeed a community of interpretation that fostered a "culture of interpretation":

> Also Jeshua, Bani, Sherebiah, Jamin, Akkub, Shabbethai, Hodiah, Maaseiah, Kelita, Azariah, Jozabad, Hanan, Pelaiah, Levites helped the people to understand the law, while the people remained in their places. So they read from the book, from the law of God, *with interpretation*. They gave the sense, so that the people understood the reading. (Neh 8:7–8)

The Jeremian tradition, then, manifests the defining transition from prophetic to scribal faith, a scribalism that would serve "the people of the scroll" and eventuated in Rabbinic instruction and interpretation.

Fourth and finally – and again – Jeremiah is, in the end, a prophet to the nations (1:5, 10). Thus far we have considered general promises of restoration of Israel, the Book of Comfort (chapters 30–31), and specific voices of Israelite hope concerning remnant kingship and scribes. All of these, in a context of displacement, depend on the defeat of Babylon as the defining political–military–theological fact of the sixth century BCE. But all of these modes of hope pertain to the faith and well-being of Israel, so that the Jeremian tradition is an intensely community-oriented tradition. Alongside that focus, however, chapter 25, perhaps the ultimate statement of hope in the Book of Jeremiah, looks past Israel and *focuses upon "all the nations"* (25:13). This apocalyptic scenario, so unlike most of the Book of Jeremiah, speaks also of "all the kingdoms" (25:26). Verses 18–25 offer an inventory of the kingdoms of the earth and imagine that all of them have been in rebellion against YHWH, the LORD of all of the nations. The message to all of the nations is, "You must drink!" (25:28). All of the nations must drink the cup of YHWH's wrath because all of them – sooner or later – must come to terms with YHWH's rule. Thus, alongside the central preoccupation of the tradition with the welfare of Israel, there is a doxological agenda of praise of YHWH, who is the creator of all of the earth and the governor of all of the peoples of the earth. Because the Jeremian tradition is situated amid the rise and fall of great powers, the tradition must attend to the ways in which the waxing and waning of worldly powers is reflective of and responsive to the sovereignty of YHWH. In this regard, the Book of Jeremiah culminates in a grand vision of the way in which all nations finally must come to terms with the rule of YHWH, the incomparable God.

YHWH's rule over the nations and YHWH's attentiveness to Israel are not in conflict, though it is clear that any given statement of the matter may tilt in one direction or the other. In this regard, the tradition is not unlike that of Exodus 14. In some verses of that chapter – those commonly regarded as coming from the Yahwistic source (Exod 14:13–14, 25, 30–31) – the key issue is *the rescue of Israel*. In the other verses, commonly regarded as belonging to the priestly source (Exod 14:4, 17), the key issue is Y<small>HWH</small>'s *grand, glorious defeat* of Pharaoh.[62] Thus, in the tradition of Jeremiah, the liberation and restoration of displaced Israel are paramount. To a large extent, the defeat of Babylon by Y<small>HWH</small> is only in the interest of Israel. But conversely, one may conclude that Israel is a small part of the large issue that Y<small>HWH</small> has with Babylon. The Book of Jeremiah, like the Old Testament generally, will not choose between these two accents. The tradition insists on holding together *cosmic sovereignty* and *covenantal fidelity*. It has belonged to the character of this God, since the disclosure to Moses, that the creator of all is the grantor of Israel:

> Now therefore, if you obey my voice and keep my covenant, you shall be my treasured possession out of all the peoples. Indeed, the whole earth is mine, but you shall be for me a priestly kingdom and a holy nation. These are the words that you shall speak to the Israelites. (Exod 19:5–6)

CONCLUSION

The task of the Jeremian tradition, from the initial summons of the prophet to the derivative traditions that constitute the book, is to articulate and enact the *reality of Y<small>HWH</small>* in a *complex, disputatious world crisis* that shattered established public order and that jeopardized the community of Israel. The variegated attempts of the tradition to maintain the connection of *Y<small>HWH</small> and crisis* require imagination in both utterance and reading. In the end, however, all of this rich variety comes to fruition in a single conviction. The future is held firmly in the hands of a *sovereign God who practices fidelity*; the future is held firmly in the hands of a *faithful God who*

---

[62] See Walter Brueggemann, "Pharaoh as Vassal: A Study of a Political Metaphor," *CBQ* 57 (1995): 27–51.

practices sovereignty. The remarkable truth of the voice of hope in the Book of Jeremiah is that this claim is made while the world is set in sickening disorder and while Israel enters an abyss, which from some angles is seen to be its termination. In that very context of rise and fall, displacement and restoration, death and new life, the tradition is unyielding in its defining connection:

> "It is I" (27:5);
> "It is he" (10:12; 51:15).

It is YHWH! It is YHWH who has called the prophet to plant and build. The planting and building takes many forms and is voiced in many images. The outcome, given poetic imagination, is not in doubt:

> Therefore, the days are surely coming, says the LORD, when it shall no longer be said, "As the LORD lives who brought the people of Israel up out of the land of Egypt," but "As the LORD lives who brought out and led the offspring of the house of Israel out of the land of the north and out of all the lands where he had driven them." Then they shall live in their own land. (Jer 23:7–8)

CHAPTER 3

The Place and Function of the Book of Jeremiah within the Old Testament

It is usual to study books of the Bible (and more specifically the Old Testament) one at a time, each as a discrete literary corpus. Thus, commentaries focus on one book at a time. That practice is further reinforced by the series in which the present volume stands, for that series – including this study of Jeremiah – proceeds "book by book." But by virtue of the canon, the books of the Bible never stand completely discrete and apart from each other. It is clear that the traditioning process that led to canon was a highly contested one in which competing voices advocated different pieces of literature. Consequently, the outcome of canon is evidently a compromise in which the various interpretive interests are juxtaposed with each other and "books" (scrolls) stand in a variety of relationships to each other. It is equally clear that such interpretive contestation is evident within many of the biblical books themselves.[1]

Our focus in this chapter is on the Book of Jeremiah as it is situated amid the other books of the canon of the Old Testament. It will be clear in this exposition that the Book of Jeremiah – rooted in *an imaginative prophet* and developed in elongated fashion by

[1] See Odil Hannes Steck, "Theological Streams of Tradition," in *Theology and Tradition in the Old Testament*, ed. Douglas A. Knight (Philadelphia: Fortress, 1977), 183–214.

134

a passionate, ongoing community of interpreters – plays a vigorous role in the interpretive contest for the future of Judaism.[2] It cannot be claimed in the end that the Book of Jeremiah is the dominant or triumphant voice in that passionate contestation; it is, however, unmistakable that the primary interpretive angle of the book, voiced by deportees in the sixth century BCE who made a decisive comeback in the fifth century BCE (see Jer 24), occupies a defining position in emerging Judaism. In what follows, I will consider the Book of Jeremiah vis-à-vis the three main parts of the canon of the Old Testament.

JEREMIAH AND THE PENTATEUCH

The Book of Jeremiah is well and knowingly situated amid the complex interpretive traditions that were eventually shaped into the Torah (Pentateuch). It is clear that the Book of Jeremiah is fully conversant with the traditions of creation (see Jer 4:23–26; 31:35–37; 33:25), the ancestors of Genesis (see Jer 33:26), the Exodus (Jer 23:7), the wilderness tradition (Jer 2:2–3), and the Sinai traditions of covenant (see Jer 7:9 for a clear citation of the decalogue as in Hos 4:2).[3] This does not mean, of course, that the Book of Jeremiah knew a fully formed Pentateuch, for that literature was being formed and developed at the same time through the same interpretive processes that produced the Book of Jeremiah. One cannot determine exactly what materials were available to the producers of the Book of Jeremiah, but only that the tradition to which

---

[2] See Christopher R. Seitz, *Theology in Conflict: Reactions to the Exile in the Book of Jeremiah*, BZAW 176 (Berlin: de Gruyter, 1989).

[3] See Walter Brueggemann, "Jeremiah: *Creatio in Extremis*," in *God Who Creates: Essays in Honor of W. Sibley Towner*, ed. William P. Brown and S. Dean McBride, Jr. (Grand Rapids, MI: Eerdmans, 2000), 152–70.

the Pentateuchal materials testify was fully accessible to and generative for the prophetic tradition. The influence is not necessarily direct or genetic but consists in what Odil Steck terms the "intellectual world" (*geistige Welt*) of the several traditions.[4]

It is the relationship of the Book of Jeremiah to the Book of Deuteronomy that has largely occupied interpreters when we inquire about links to the Pentateuch. There can be no doubt that the Book of Jeremiah is intimately related to the Book of Deuteronomy. The Book of Deuteronomy is a product of a passionate, tenacious interpretive community in the eighth–seventh centuries BCE that recast the faith of Israel with reminiscences of Sinai. That memory was forged into a vigorous covenantal theology that focused on the exclusive demands of YHWH voiced in commandments (Deut 12–25) and on the sanctions of blessing and curse (Deut 28). The tight connection between *commandments* and *sanctions* yields a symmetrical formulation of "life or death" according to obedience or disobedience of the Torah:

> See, I have set before you today life and prosperity, death and adversity. If you obey the commandments of the LORD your God that I am commanding you today, by loving the LORD your God, walking in his ways, and observing his commandments, decrees, and ordinances, then you shall live and become numerous, and the LORD your God will bless you in the land that you are entering to possess. But if your heart turns away and you do not hear, but are led astray to bow down to other gods and serve them, I declare to you today that you shall perish; you shall not live long in the land that you are crossing the Jordan to enter and possess. I call heaven and earth to witness against you today that I have set before you life and death, blessings and curses. Choose life so that you and your descendants

---

[4] Steck, "Theological Streams of Tradition," 186.

may live, loving the LORD your God, obeying him, and holding fast to him; for that means life to you and length of days, so that you may live in the land that the LORD swore to give to your ancestors, to Abraham, to Isaac, and to Jacob. (Deut 30:15–20)[5]

In its most reified form, this theology in the tradition of Deuteronomy allowed for very little slippage (grace, forgiveness) because the jealous, exclusive claims of YHWH are known to be uncompromising. For our purposes, it is important to observe that this covenantal theology acknowledged kingship in one important instruction (Deut 17:14–20) but in reality allowed monarchy to have no independent claim on YHWH and reduced the king to one more Israelite who was subject to Torah obedience (see 1 Sam 12:14–15, 25). It is fair to say that this theology came to be the dominant theology of the covenant that eventually funded both Judaism and Christianity.

Of special consequence for Israel's theological life is, as already mentioned, the emergence of another vigorous theological stream, the Deuteronomic–Deuteronomistic tradition. An occurrence with great significance for the history of literature accounts for this. After 722 BCE, the oral and written texts from the Northern kingdom, together with their traditionists, entered the land of Judah, were accepted there, and apparently set in motion a process that reinforced a specifically Israelite consciousness of being the people of Israel. This awareness was to prove very significant for Israel's identity in the following period, when every political reference for Israel

---

[5] See my discussion of this theology under the rubric of "Structure Legitimation" in Walter Brueggemann, "A Shape for Old Testament Theology I: Structure Legitimation," *CBQ* 47 (1985): 28–46, reprinted in *Old Testament Theology: Essays on Structure, Theme, and Text,* ed. Patrick D. Miller (Minneapolis: Fortress, 1992), 1–21.

crumbled and the universal claims of the Jerusalem cult tradition were placed in radical question. The prophetic traditions (including Hosea) from the Northern kingdom; the narrative traditions about the judges, Samuel, and Saul; and the Elohistic narrative are significant components in this Judean process of activating Israel's early historical traditions and the Israelite self-understanding connected with these traditions.[6]

Around the crisis of the sixth century BCE, however, this tight, symmetrical, uncompromising theology of blessing and curse (life or death) could not be sustained in a simplistic form. Thus, the interpretive trajectory of Deuteronomy in the sixth century had to offer some grounds for a new possibility after failure; it did so by adjusting the tight symmetry of the covenant to allow for repentance and a return to covenantal obedience. This interpretive development, required by circumstance and carried out in an imaginative way, is reflected in Deuteronomy 4:29–31 and 30:1–10, in Jeremiah 29:10–14, and in 1 Kings 8:31–46.[7] The same interpretive trajectory is reflected, moreover, in the remarkable teaching of Ezekiel 18 that allows a new generation (the generation of exiles in the sixth century) to move beyond the antecedent death sentence of its predecessors in order to resume a life of obedience.[8]

It is evident from all this that the tradition of Deuteronomy is a broad, sustained theological trajectory over several generations that had the interpretive imagination to respond to and adjust to new circumstances in a way that allowed theological innovation

[6]Steck, "Theological Streams of Tradition," 203–4.

[7]See Hans Walter Wolff, "The Kerygma of the Deuteronomic Historical Work," in *The Vitality of Old Testament Tradition*, ed. Walter Brueggemann and Hans Walter Wolff, 2nd ed. (Atlanta: John Knox, 1982), 83–100.

[8]See Paul Joyce, *Divine Initiative and Human Response in Ezekiel*, JSOTSup 51 (Sheffield: JSOT Press, 1989), 33–87.

while maintaining a core of interpretive continuity. The Deutero-nomic tradition of theology thus is to be understood not simply as the production of a "book" but as reflecting a deeply passion-ate circle of interpreters sustained over several generations. That circle focused their articulation of Israel's faith on the exclusive claim of YHWH as the LORD of the covenant and, correlatively, on Israel's singular vocation of obedience to covenantal command-ments. Robert R. Wilson is surely correct in seeing the literary evidence as testimony to the sociological force and reality of a community of interpreters over time that represented deeply held theological views with immense public implications.[9] And yet, over time, this view of YHWH's exclusive claim of sovereignty was bound to collide with the high royal temple claims of Jerusalem. That colli-sion inevitably cast the Deuteronomic "stream of tradition" as one in opposition to the assumed autonomy of Jerusalem under the unconditional patronage of YHWH. This Deuteronomic theology cast a firm "if" of conditionality over the life and faith of Jerusalem, a conditionality intolerable to the high theological pretensions of Jerusalem.[10]

It has long been known that the prose sections of Jeremiah have much in common with the rhetoric and theological assumptions of the tradition of Deuteronomy.[11] This is evident in particular rhetorical cadences but it is also unmistakable in the larger claims of

---

[9] Robert R. Wilson, *Prophecy and Society in Ancient Israel* (Philadelphia: Fortress, 1980).

[10] The conditional "if" recurs in many places in the Deuteronomic literature. Most spectacularly, it stands at the beginning of the great Sinai proclamation of Exodus 19:5–6.

[11] See J. Philip Hyatt, "Jeremiah and Deuteronomy," *JNES* 1 (1942): 156–73; and H. H. Rowley, "The Prophet Jeremiah and the Book of Deuteronomy," in *Studies in Old Testament Prophecy*, ed. H. H. Rowley (Edinburgh: T. and T. Clark, 1950), 157–74.

covenantal theology as is made clear, for example, in Jeremiah 11:1–17 with its advocacy of "covenant" (v. 2) and a preoccupation with the burden of listening and obeying (vv. 4, 8).[12] It is thus plausible to suggest that the prose material in Jeremiah to no small degree reflects Deuteronomic theology. Although the connections of the poetic materials of Jeremiah to Deuteronomy are not as obvious, it is nevertheless likely that the poetic speeches of judgment – including indictment and sentence – which are expressed with enormous freedom and imagination, reflect the same covenantal insistence and reflect the agenda of Deuteronomy concerning the exclusive claims of Yhwh.

As the Book of Deuteronomy reflects a necessary development from harsh symmetry to permit forgiveness and return, so the prose of Jeremiah also allows for repentance (*šûb*) in a way that serves to move beyond the harsh closure of much of the prophetic poetry:

> It may be that they will listen, all of them, and will *turn* [*wĕyāšūbû*] from their evil way, that I may change my mind about the disaster that I intend to bring on them because of their evil doings. (Jer 26:3)

> It may be that when the house of Judah hears of all the disasters that I intend to do to them, all of them may *turn* [*yāšûbû*] from their evil ways, so that I may forgive their iniquity and their sin. (Jer 36:3)

In the prophetic tradition as in the Torah tradition, even the firm, nearly absolute claims of covenant must adapt to the lived circumstance of the community. Ernest W. Nicholson has considered in some detail this latter development in both traditions and has exhibited in a compelling way the remarkable juxtaposition

---

[12] Hyatt, "Jeremiah and Deuteronomy," 168, comments: "Chapter 11 is *crux interpretem* in the study of our problem."

of 2 Kings 22 and Jeremiah 36, both reflections of developed Deuteronomistic theology.[13] In 2 Kings 22, the response of the good king Josiah to the scroll just discovered (apparently the scroll of Deuteronomy) is to repent and institute reform. By contrast, the bad king Jehoiakim in Jeremiah 36 seeks to destroy the scroll and thereby to eliminate its author, giving no hint of repentance. These two texts together exhibit the way in which the same *theology of scroll* – for life or for death, for blessing or for curse – operates in both traditions. It is clear that Josiah, the key character in the narrative of 2 Kings 22, is the champion Torah-keeper in the Deuteronomistic history; notice should particularly be taken of the poetry in Jeremiah 22:15–16, wherein the prophetic texts contrast the good king and father Josiah with the bad king and son Jehoiakim.[14] Josiah is celebrated as a Torah-keeper who attended to the poor and needy by doing justice, exactly what Deuteronomy intends for kingship:

> When he has taken the throne of his kingdom, he shall have a copy of this law written for him in the presence of the levitical priests. It shall remain with him and he shall read in it all the days of his life, so that he may learn to fear the LORD his God, diligently observing all the words of this law and these statutes. (Deut 17:18–19)

Thus we are able to see that even in the poetry of Jeremiah, the starchy insistence of Deuteronomy is at work. The evidence is compelling that in the Book of Jeremiah there is both originary poetry and later prose theological interpretation that stayed very close to the covenantal commitments of Deuteronomy.

---

[13] Ernest W. Nicholson, *Preaching to the Exiles: A Study of the Prose Tradition in the Book of Jeremiah* (Oxford: Blackwell, 1970).

[14] See Rowley, "The Prophet Jeremiah and the Book of Deuteronomy," 161–68, for an accent on the cruciality of Josiah.

Exactly how we are to understand the connection of Jeremiah to Deuteronomy is not clear. When one asks historical questions as scholars are wont to do, questions of chronology dominate concerning the exact dating of Jeremiah's work in relationship to the reform of Josiah or to the initial presentation of Deuteronomistic history. Conversely, when one asks literary questions, issues arise concerning literary dependence in a way that is sometimes reduced to "scissors and paste." My own judgment is that Wilson's sociological perspective is most helpful.[15] That work permits us to consider that the ongoing community of interpretation we dub "Deuteronomic" was a sustained, intentional voice of opposition in Jerusalem that included scribes (Baruch, Seriah), powerful public figures (Shaphan and his family), and perhaps Jeremiah, who functions as an articulator, albeit with enormous imaginative freedom, for this rigorous covenantal theology.

This convergence would also explain the continuing development of the Book of Jeremiah long after the person of Jeremiah. It also suggests that Deuteronomic theology is not imposed on the work of Jeremiah but is in fact intrinsic to it. Thus, in very different forms, both the poetry and the prose in the Book of Jeremiah reflect a demanding covenantal theology that would reread contemporary life according to the categories of covenant as construed in Deuteronomy. Taken in this way, Deuteronomy and Jeremiah together form an axis of interpretation that is central to the Old Testament and that offers a primary alternative to the dominant institutional forms of monarchy and temple in Jerusalem. The resilient nature of this interpretive axis is evident when we consider that the dominant institutional forms of faith in Jerusalem were all swept away; the community was then left with a conviction about the

---

[15] Wilson, *Prophecy and Society in Ancient Israel*, 231–51.

covenant, a vocation of obedience, and an ongoing enterprise of interpretation – precisely what is given to us in Deuteronomy and Jeremiah.

Granting the deep connection between Deuteronomy and Jeremiah, one other comment is necessary. While Deuteronomy developed a possibility of *restoration through repentance*, it continued to insist that a *return to obedience* is the precondition for the future. The tradition of Deuteronomy did not go beyond this hope. By contrast, the ongoing tradition of Jeremiah broke decisively with that conditionality; in its later statement, it was able to voice divine forgiveness without the condition of obedience (Jer 31:34; 33:8).[16] This remarkable development toward a theology of grace manifests the way in which the tradition of Jeremiah is amazingly supple, even beyond its roots in Deuteronomic circles.

JEREMIAH AND THE PROPHETS

Jeremiah and the Deuteronomistic History

We may consider this theme in relation to two subsections of "prophetic books" in the Hebrew canon, the "Former Prophets" and the "Latter Prophets."[17] The "Former Prophets" consist of Joshua, Judges, Samuel, and Kings and are commonly judged to be an expression of Deuteronomic theology. Thus, much of what was said about Deuteronomy also applies here concerning Jeremiah's relationship to the Deuteronomistic corpus of Joshua, Judges,

---

[16] See Walter Brueggemann, "The Travail of Pardon: Reflections on *slḥ*," in *A God So Near: Essays on Old Testament Theology in Honor of Patrick D. Miller*, ed. Brent A. Strawn and Nancy R. Bowen (Winona Lake, IN: Eisenbrauns, 2003), 283–97.

[17] See Walter Brueggemann, *An Introduction to the Old Testament: The Canon and Christian Imagination* (Louisville, KY: Westminster John Knox, 2003), 101–8.

Samuel, and Kings. It is variously judged by scholars that the corpus was written near the end of the seventh and into the sixth century BCE – somewhere related to the death of Josiah (609 BCE), the fall of Jerusalem (587 BCE), and the final note on Jehoiachin (562 BCE).[18] In other words, this corpus was shaped and written during the period of the dynamism of the Jeremian tradition. It was written, according to common interpretation, to trace the failed history of Israel from the moment it entered the land (Joshua 1–4) until the final destruction of 587 BCE at the hands of the Babylonians – one long tale of *disobedience* that led inexorably to *destruction*.

It is easy to see that Jeremiah lives in the "intellectual world" of such a narrative, for the Jeremian tradition also traces the inexorable account of the destruction of Jerusalem.[19] In the Deuteronomistic history, the final destruction of Jerusalem is narrated in 2 Kings 24:10–25:26. In the same way, judgment against Jerusalem is evident, albeit in a somewhat different form, in Jeremiah 21:3–7; 27:5–22; 37:17–21; 38:14–28; and particularly 52:1–27, where the same material from 2 Kings is reiterated. The narrative rendition of Jeremiah is congruent with the account in the Book of Kings, for the prophetic tradition, even while taking account of historical specificity, gives testimony to YHWH's rule in public history.

The point is less clear in the poetry of Jeremiah, but one can readily detect points of contact with this same version of inexorable destruction.

First, in Jeremiah 2:5–8, Jerusalem is indicted because it forgot the "credo tradition" that testifies to the gift of the land (see Josh

---

[18] See Walter Brueggemann, *Reverberations of Faith: A Theological Handbook of Old Testament Themes* (Louisville, KY: Westminster John Knox, 2002), 52–55, and the bibliography noted there.

[19] On the phrase "intellectual world," see Steck, "Theological Streams of Tradition," 186.

4:22–24). When the tradition is disregarded, the outcome is a kind of "forgetting" that is featured in the core section of the Book of Judges. As Israel is said to worship "Baal and Asherah" (Judg 3:7), so the prophet indicts those who "prophesy for Baal" (Jer 2:8). The long Deuteronomic account surfaces in fragments in the prophetic poetry.

Second, the prophet indicts Jerusalem for waywardness "from your youth":

> I spoke to you in your prosperity,
> but you said, "I will not listen."
> This has been your way from your youth,
> for you have not obeyed my voice. (Jer 22:21)

* * *

> For after I had turned away I repented;
> and after I was discovered, I struck my thigh;
> I was ashamed, and I was dismayed
> because I bore the disgrace of my youth.
> (Jer 31:19; see in prose 3:25, 32:30)

The phrase "from your youth" surely means that Israel's waywardness is from the beginning. In Deuteronomistic perspective, that claim likely means on land entry. This conception of Israel's history of waywardness that evokes divine wrath is congruent with the account of the Deuteronomistic history.

Third, the famous rhetorical question of Jeremiah 13:23 reflects the conviction that Israel has been recalcitrant forever and that Israel will remain recalcitrant:

> Can Ethiopians change their skin
> or leopards their spots?
> Then also you can do good
> who are accustomed to do evil. (Jer 13:23)

This question coheres with the Deuteronomistic judgment that the entire history of Israel (Joshua, Judges, Samuel, Kings) is the history of disobedience that leads, inescapably, to exile:

> I will scatter you like chaff
> driven by the wind from the desert. (Jer 13:24)

And the reason for the coming destruction is, yet again, "forgetting" (see Jer 13:25).

A second point of contact between Deuteronomistic history and Jeremiah is the crucial role played by Josiah in the Deuteronomistic narrative (2 Kings 22–23). Josiah is the model Torah-keeping king (see Deut 17:14–20), and it is the royal Torah-keeping that constitutes the only chance for Jerusalem's future. As noted, Jeremiah also regards Josiah as the model king (Jer 22:15–16) and likely aligns himself with the royal reform (see Jer 11:1–8). Thus, the two pieces of literature surely inhabit the same world of theological passion concerning "plucking up and tearing down."

Jeremiah among the Prophets

The matter of Jeremiah's connection with the *Latter Prophets* (Isaiah, Ezekiel, and the Twelve) is a good deal more complex. There is no doubt that the books of each of the "major prophets," Isaiah, Jeremiah, and Ezekiel, developed in their own way, in a particular context and according to a particular stream of tradition. Nonetheless, as Ronald E. Clements has noted, there is, in all of these prophetic books, a powerful impetus toward thematization that orders the several rhetorical units around the issue of *displacement and restoration*.[20] There is no doubt that this thematization

---

[20] Ronald E. Clements, "Patterns in the Prophetic Canon," in *Canon and Authority: Essays on Old Testament Religion and Theology*, ed. George W. Coats and Burke O. Long (Philadelphia: Fortress, 1977), 42–55.

is a process that was preoccupied with the crisis of Jerusalem, the same issue that, of course, preoccupied the Jeremian tradition. Thus, the Book of Isaiah in its two parts, chapters 1–39 and 40–66, concerned the "old things" of judgment and the "new thing" of restoration.[21] The Book of Ezekiel is even more symmetrically ordered, with chapters 1–24 as judgment and chapters 25–48 as anticipated restoration. The Book of Jeremiah shares this schema, though the exact interface between the two themes is not as clear in the Book of Jeremiah as it is in the books of Isaiah and Ezekiel. In general, we may say that after chapter 28, the Book of Jeremiah focuses on the future, though the most powerful statements of promise are clustered, as we have seen, in chapters 30–33. Reference to Isaiah and Ezekiel can instruct us in the thematization of Jeremiah and helps us to focus on the two fundamental theological motifs of YHWH *as promise-maker* and YHWH *as future-giver.*

Inside that general thematization, it is possible to appreciate some distinctions and variations among the prophets. As noted, Hananiah in Jeremiah 28 echoes the high Zion theology of the Isaiah tradition that is given impetus by the delivery of Jerusalem from the Assyrians in 701 BCE. Although Jeremiah is a century after Isaiah, it is clear that Jeremiah represents a deep challenge to the Zion theology championed by the Isaianic tradition and echoed by Hananiah. In Ezekiel 36, the possibility of a future for Jerusalem is grounded in YHWH's self-regard and not in any commitment to Israel:

> Therefore say to the house of Israel, Thus says the LORD God: It is not for your sake, O house of Israel, that I am about to act, but for the sake of my holy name, which you have profaned among the nations to which you came. (Ezek 36:22; see also v. 32)

---

[21] See Brevard S. Childs, *Introduction to the Old Testament as Scripture* (Philadelphia: Fortress, 1979), 325–33.

This is in marked contrast with the grounding of the future in Yhwh's passionate love for Israel in the tradition of Jeremiah:

> I have loved you with an everlasting love. (Jer 31:3b)

* * *

> Is Ephraim my dear son?
> Is he the child I delight in?
> As often as I speak against him,
> I still remember him.
> Therefore I am deeply moved for him;
> I will surely have mercy on him,
> says the LORD. (Jer 31:20)

Thus Jeremiah's articulation of Yhwh's *pathos* is quite in contrast to Ezekiel's accent on austere *holiness*.[22] The scribal juxtaposition of the prophetic materials in the present shape of the canon causes us to notice both the immense range and variation in the prophets, even given the common thematization, and the peculiar accents of the Jeremian tradition, which, as Abraham J. Heschel has shown, go more deeply into divine pathos than does any other prophetic tradition.

The question of the thematic unity of the *twelve minor prophets*, whose works occupy a single scroll, is still only beginning to be discussed by scholars. It seems likely, nonetheless, that we may see that the Book of the Twelve is also thematized around issues of judgment and restoration. As a result, as one moves through from Hosea to Malachi, one can see a shift from speeches of judgment to

---

[22] Whereas Jeremiah receives extended discussion in Abraham J. Heschel, *The Prophets* (New York: Harper and Row, 1962), Ezekiel is almost absent. In a book about divine pathos, this disregard of Ezekiel is a most important datum.

oracles of promise.[23] So also in the Twelve, the same thematization so crucial to the Book of Jeremiah is evident.

That being granted, it is still quite useful, in reflecting on the "minor prophets," to consider them one at a time in historical-critical fashion. When we consider them in this way, we may take note of four of these prophets in particular.

THE BOOK OF HOSEA. Of all of the prophetic traditions, Jeremiah stands closest to and most in debt to Hosea. Hosea lived and spoke a century before Jeremiah and seems to belong to the traditions that were antecedent to Deuteronomy. Like Jeremiah after him, Hosea employed immense poetic imagination in order to redescribe the public crises of his time – the incursion of Assyria, the Syro-Ephraimite War, and the jeopardy of Samaria – in terms of the rule of YHWH.

To that end, Hosea, like Jeremiah after him, used character-istic prophetic genres of speech. He did so, again in anticipa-tion of Jeremiah, with enormous freedom. Whereas the speeches of judgment in Amos and Micah are vigorous and disciplined, Hosea's judgment-speech characteristically exhibits great freedom and imagination in articulation.[24] The "spine" of indictment and sentence are visible in Hosea but not in a flat and direct way. Hosea's capacity for promissory oracle, moreover, evidences the same Yahwistic "leap" beyond judgment that we have seen in Jeremiah.

---

[23] See Paul R. House, *The Unity of the Twelve*, JSOTSup 97, BLS 27 (Sheffield: Almond, 1990); and James D. Nogalski and Marvin A. Sweeney, eds., *Reading and Hearing the Book of the Twelve*, SBLSymS 15 (Atlanta: Society of Biblical Literature, 2000).

[24] On the prophetic judgment-speech, see Claus Westermann, *Basic Forms of Prophetic Speech* (Philadelphia: Westminster, 1967).

Hosea's capacity for image and metaphor is remarkable when compared with other contemporary prophetic rhetoric. Thus Yahwistic destructiveness is as a ravenous lion (Hos 5:14–15); the rebellious political conduct of the community is "hot as an oven" (7:7); Ephraim, in its political vacillation, is "half-baked," too heated on one side, undercooked on the other (7:8); Israel is as desperate and frantic as an anxious, trapped dove flying to and fro (7:11); Israel is like a vine (10:1); and Ephraim is like a disobedient heifer, now put to hard work (10:11). This rich inventory of images is extraordinary as the poet strains to bring to speech the extremity of Israel's crisis.

The richness of imagery and the employment of characteristic prophetic genres are in the service of *covenant theology,* for Hosea makes clear, like none before him, that the YHWH–Israel relationship is an exclusive loyalty expressed as glad, trusting obedience. With that premise, the prophet then proceeds to show that the covenant is broken and that the covenant-breaking community is in deep jeopardy. It is noteworthy that this act of prophetic imagination is able to subsume all of the contemporary international reality and the internal life of Israel in this all-defining relationship. This venturesome imagery in the service of the covenant is pushed further by Hosea than by anyone before him:

> It is Hosea who flashes a glimpse into the inner life of God as he ponders his relationship to Israel.[25]

It is this capacity to enter into the internal life of YHWH and bring it to speech that makes Hosea distinctive in the prophetic tradition. Hosea is able to show that YHWH is no "principle of justice," no "remote sovereign," but a deeply engaged partner who is so invested

---

[25] Heschel, *The Prophets,* 47.

in the covenantal relationship that this relationship proves costly for Yнwн. Thus the poet articulates the deep passion and vulnerability of Yнwн that moves in poetic intimacy rather than in the cold formality of speeches of judgment.

The prophet is able to speak of and exhibit Yнwн in this way because of the utilization of familial (as distinct from political) images. For example, in Hosea 2, the long, dramatic poem moves from divorce (vv. 2–13) to remarriage (vv. 14–25), as the prophet is able to imagine the relationship through the crisis.[26] In parallel fashion, in Hosea 11:1–9, the poet utilizes parental imagery and presents a parent in crisis for a growing child. In both texts, with images of marriage and parenthood, the prophet reflects on Yнwн's risk in the relationship. In chapter 2, a leap is made from verse 13 to verse 14 because Yнwн is "God and not man" and will act differently in the yearning for a restored relationship. In 11:1–7, the parent speaks and, in the move from verse 7 to verse 8, makes a leap of anguish for the sake of the relationship. Thus a prophet renders the *covenant* in terms of *intimate, interpersonal* anguish and possibility:

> Hosea reaches an awareness of the basic feeling, of the latent sub-jective meaning in all individual announcements and decisions. We hear not merely of an incidental pathos, but also of the car-dinal, fundamental emotion; not merely of particular attitudes, but also of the constitutive relationship between God and Israel. Over and above the immediate and contingent emotional reaction of the LORD we are informed about an eternal and basic disposition. The historically conditioned expressions of pathos and the immediate situation between God and man are set in the light of the eternal background. . . . To Hosea, marriage is the image for the relationship of God and Israel. This is one of the boldest conceptions of religious

---

[26]See Heschel, *The Prophets*, on the dramatic force of this text.

thinking. It may lack the excitement of adventure, but it has the aura of sublimity. It involves restraint, bringing with it duties and responsibilities, but it also endows with a nobility that is a synonym for eternity. Israel is the consort of God.[27]

By the time Hosea finishes, the covenant is no longer simply a formal requirement for Israel; now it is an engagement in which Yhwh is at risk. It is, moreover, Yhwh's being at risk that makes the leap to newness possible, as we have seen in the leap from Jer 30:15 to 30:16. Hosea has evidently instructed Jeremiah in the possibility of presenting the covenant in images that seem, on the face of it, ill-suited to a disciplined relationship. Such a utilization of imagery makes a broken covenant unbearable; it is, however, that same articulation of pathos through marital and parental imagery that makes newness and restoration possible in a context where Israel is wholly undeserving. Jeremiah thus inherits from Hosea *the mystery of newness wrought through anguish,* or as we may say in the Christian tradition, *life wrought out of death.* Thus the very prophet who probes most deeply the interpersonal *anguish* of the covenant is the one who can most wondrously speak about *newness*:

> Now I will uncover her shame
> in the sight of her lovers,
> and no one shall rescue her
> out of my hand.
> I will put an end to all her mirth,
> her festivals, her new moons,
> her Sabbaths,
> and all her appointed festivals.
> I will lay waste her vines and her fig trees,
> of which she said,
> "These are my pay,

---

[27] Ibid., 48, 50.

which my lovers have given me."
I will make them a forest,
and the wild animals shall devour them.
I will punish her for the festival days of the Baals,
when she offered incense to them
and decked herself with her ring and jewelry,
and went after her lovers,
and forgot me, says the LORD.
Therefore, I will now allure her,
and bring her into the wilderness,
and speak tenderly to her.
From there I will give her her vineyards,
and make the Valley of Achor a door of hope. (Hos 2:10–14)

And I will take you for my wife forever; I will take you for my wife
in righteousness and in justice, in steadfast love, and in mercy. I will
take you for my wife in faithfulness; and you shall know the LORD.
(Hos 2:19–20)

A century later, Jeremiah has learned from Hosea the mystery of
the covenant as a passion of love that has the capacity to go deep
into suffering and alienation and then to find energy, freedom, and
resolve to generate a newness that moves beyond the rupture of
infidelity. Hosea has moved beyond the rupture of infidelity in the
leap of passion:

> How can I give you up, Ephraim?
> How can I hand you over, O Israel?
> How can I make you like Admah?
> How can I treat you like Zeboiim?
> My heart recoils within me;
> my compassion grows warm and tender.
> I will not execute my fierce anger;
> I will not again destroy Ephraim;
> for I am God and no mortal,
> the Holy One in your midst,
> and I will not come in wrath. (Hos 11:8–9)

A century later, Jeremiah has brought to speech the God who moves from "plucking up and tearing down" to "planting and building":

> And just as I have watched over them to pluck up and break down, to overthrow, destroy, and bring evil, so I will watch over them to build and to plant, says the LORD. (Jer 31:28)

Such a move depends on a God of pathos who in candor and yearning generates newness beyond alienation – this is the God of Hosea and the God of Jeremiah.

THE BOOK OF OBADIAH. The Oracles Against the Nations in chapters 46–51, in the LXX situated amid chapter 25, exhibit the Book of Jeremiah enacting the prophetic vocation to be a "prophet to the nations" (1:5, 10). That vocation pertains especially to Babylon, and the final Oracle Against the Nations in chapters 50–51 articulates the accent that is so decisive for the rhetorical, theological strategy of the Book of Jeremiah.[28] Preceding the oracle against Babylon in chapters 50–51 are a series of shorter oracles pertaining to "lesser nations," nations less powerful and less central to Jeremiah's concern.

Here I mention only the oracle against Edom in Jeremiah 49:7–22, which consists of a complex series of rhetorical fragments. The oracle, in its unmitigated statement of divine harshness, reflects Judah's abiding and here intensified antipathy toward Edom. The oracle has close parallels in the Book of Obadiah in its rhetorical assault on Edom. Specifically, Jeremiah 49:14–16 is closely paralleled in Obadiah 1–5. It is impossible to determine the direction of literary

---

[28] See John Hill, *Friend or Foe? The Figure of Babylon in the Book of Jeremiah*, BIS 40 (Leiden: Brill, 1999).

dependence. It is most plausible to regard both oracles as usages of a common piece of oracular practice that pertained to Yhwh's judgment on the nations in general and on Edom in particular. While Obadiah can provide an indictment as grounds for the harsh judgment (see Obad 10–14; cf. Amos 1:11–12), and while Obadiah concludes with an affirmative comment on Zion and its restoration, the oracle in Jeremiah 49 lacks these notes and one-dimensionally focuses on divine judgment.

This close parallel between Jeremiah and Obadiah helps us to situate the developing Jeremian tradition (beyond the time of Jeremiah) in a way that is representative and characteristic of prophetic utterance. The Jeremian tradition draws on a common stock of Oracles Against the Nations.[29] This common stock, of which the Jeremian tradition is a powerful representative, exhibits the "metahistory" of Yhwh's governance;[30] notice the use of the characteristic terms "plan" and "purpose" whereby Yhwh governs:

> Therefore hear *the plan* that the LORD has made against Edom and the *purposes* that he has formed against the inhabitants of Teman: Surely the little ones of the flock shall be dragged away; surely their fold shall be appalled at their fate. (Jer 49:20)[31]

John Barton may be correct to suggest – on the basis of Amos 1–2 – that this sense of Yhwh's governance is linked to a kind of "natural law" that reflects Yhwh as creator but does not appeal

---

[29] See Douglas Stuart, *Hosea-Jonah*, WBC 31 (Waco, TX: Word, 1987), 405–6.

[30] On "metahistory," see Klaus Koch, *The Prophets I: The Assyrian Period* (Philadelphia: Fortress, 1983), 5, 73, 88, 99, 156, and passim.

[31] Concerning the "divine plan," see Walter Brueggemann, "Planned People/Planned Book?" in *Writing and Reading the Scroll of Isaiah: Studies of an Interpretive Tradition*, ed. Craig C. Broyles and Craig A. Evans, 2 vols., VTSup 70 (Leiden: Brill, 1997), 1:19–37.

to Sinai commands.[32] Thus the connection of Jeremiah with the Obadiah tradition attests to the prophetic horizon that looks to world governance that concerns all nations, even if that governance is initially conducted from Jerusalem.[33]

THE BOOK OF JONAH. The late prophetic narrative of the Book of Jonah articulates a theology of *repentance* that is especially congruent with the book and the Book of Deuteronomy and its traditions. But because the Book of Jeremiah participates more fully in that theology of repentance, we may suggest that the Book of Jonah reflects only one aspect of the Book of Jeremiah.[34]

The narrative of Jonah concerns YHWH's judgment against Assyria (Nineveh) (1:2; 3:1–4), Nineveh's repentance (3:5–9), and Jonah's negative reaction to YHWH's forgiveness of Nineveh (4:1–3). The thrust of the narrative, as it concerns us, is that even the hated, feared kingdom of Assyria can be forgiven by YHWH of its great wickedness when it repents. Everything turns on the readiness of Assyria and its king to repent, a motif evident, as we have noted, in Deuteronomy 4:29–31, 30:1–10, and 1 Kings 8:33–53:

> And the people of Nineveh believed God; they proclaimed a fast, and everyone, great and small, put on sackcloth. When the news reached the king of Nineveh, he rose from his throne, removed his robe, covered himself with sackcloth, and sat in ashes. Then he had a proclamation made in Nineveh: "By the decree of the king and

---

[32] John Barton, *Understanding Old Testament Ethics: Approaches and Explorations* (Louisville, KY: Westminster John Knox, 2003), 77–129.

[33] On the Jerusalem focus of such a vision, see Norman K. Gottwald, *All the Kingdoms of the Earth: Israelite Prophecy and International Relations in the Ancient Near East* (New York: Harper and Row, 1964), 196–203.

[34] For the accent on repentance in the book of Jeremiah, see William L. Holladay, *The Root šûbh in the Old Testament with Particular Reference to Its Usages in Covenantal Contexts* (Leiden: Brill, 1958).

his nobles: No human being or animal, no herd or flock, shall taste anything. They shall not feed, nor shall they drink water. Human beings and animals shall be covered with sackcloth, and they shall cry mightily to God. All shall turn from their evil ways and from the violence that is in their hands. Who knows? God may relent and change his mind; he may turn from his fierce anger, so that we do not perish." (Jon 3:5–9)

The divine response to repentance is a decisive inversion of divine intention:

When God saw what they did, how they turned from their evil ways, God changed his mind about the calamity that he had said he would bring upon them; and he did not do it. (Jon 3:10)

The prophetic message is that repentance permits restoration of life under Yhwh's governance.

Beyond the general theme of repentance, this teaching has direct and immediate parallels with the teaching of Jeremiah 18:7–10:

At one moment I may declare concerning a nation or a kingdom, that I will pluck up and break down and destroy it, but if that nation, concerning which I have spoken, turns from its evil, I will change my mind about the disaster that I intended to bring on it. And at another moment I may declare concerning a nation or a kingdom that I will build and plant it, but if it does evil in my sight, not listening to my voice, then I will change my mind about the good that I had intended to do to it. (Jer 18:7–10)

The remarkable assertion is that *human response* evokes *divine change*. This connection indicates that the human subject (Jerusalem for Jeremiah, Nineveh for Jonah) can indeed choose its own future by making an appropriate response to Yhwh. Neither Jerusalem nor Nineveh is fated to judgment and destruction. The narrative of Jonah provides a case study of that theological conviction. In the case of Jeremiah, of course, such a "turn" was not forthcoming:

> Now, therefore, say to the people of Judah and the inhabitants of Jerusalem: Thus says the LORD: Look, I am a potter shaping evil against you and devising a plan against you. Turn now, all of you from your evil way, and amend your ways and your doings.
>
> But they say, "It is no use! We will follow our own plans, and each of us will act according to the stubbornness of our evil will." (Jer 18:11–12)

As a consequence, YHWH did not change and Jerusalem received the judgment already declared – "namely,"

> I will pluck up and break down and destroy. (Jer 18:7)

The example of the narrative of Jonah evidences that the theology of repentance propagated by Deuteronomy and voiced in the Jeremian tradition was indeed current in the sixth century BCE. That theology provided hope even in acute crisis. Beyond that, the usage testifies to a deeply engaged God who operates with freedom appropriate to a serious and lively relationship. In some texts of Jeremiah, it was too late for "return." In this instance, however, it is late but not too late.[35]

THE BOOK OF AMOS. The Book of Amos, like every prophetic tradition, is complex in its formation. Hans Walter Wolff hypothesizes six strata in the editorial process of the book, whereas

---

[35] A. Vanlier Hunter, in his *Seek the LORD! A Study of the Meaning and Function of the Exhortations in Amos, Hosea, Isaiah, Micah, and Zephaniah* (Baltimore: St. Mary's Seminary and University, 1982), has shown how the prophets urge to repent but then characteristically announce that it is too late for turning. He does not, however, discuss the Jeremian tradition.

Robert B. Coote proposes three stages.[36] Both Wolff and Coote propose a "Deuteronomic edition" of the Book of Amos that updates the words of Amos for a later time and that reasserts the crucial choice that God's people must make yet again.[37] In Coote's conceptualization:

> The B stage *re*offers the crucial choice of Deut. 30:19: "I have set before you life and death, blessing and curse; therefore choose life, that you and your descendants may live." If an event described in Deut. 28:15–68 should occur, as several do in Amos 4:6–11, it is a warning rather than a final curse. For Amos, God has chosen. For the B stage, the people are to choose. For Amos, God chose curse because the people had chosen transgression. For the B stage, the people's choice is open again. Amos bound a future to a past. The B stage focuses squarely on the present. Whereas Amos said in effect, "You have not set justice in the gate; therefore I will destroy you," the B stage says, "Set justice in the gate" (5:15).
>
> There are further hints of the similarity of the B-stage passages mentioned in this section to the deuteronomistic tradition.[38]

This proposed stratum of traditioning pertains to Deuteronomy and not directly to Jeremiah, except that this way of thinking is directly congenial to the issues in Jeremiah:

> The oracle against Judah is an obvious choice for updating the set to take into account the Babylonian exile. Its language is prosaic, extremely general, and emphasizes idolatry, like the second, or exilic, edition of the Deuteronomistic History (Dtr 2). For the C editor, insofar as Judah takes Israel's place as the culminating oracle, the

---

[36] Hans Walter Wolff, *Joel and Amos: A Commentary on the Books of the Prophets Joel and Amos*, Hermeneia (Philadelphia: Fortress, 1977), 106–13; Robert B. Coote, *Amos among the Prophets* (Philadelphia: Fortress, 1981).

[37] Wolff, *Joel and Amos*, 112–13; Coote, *Amos among the Prophets*, 46–109.

[38] Coote, *Amos among the Prophets*, 60.

earlier group of "example" nations is reorganized to center Tyre and Edom:

$\left\{\begin{array}{l}\text{Aram} \\ \text{Philistia}\end{array}\right.$

Tyre

Edom

$\left\{\begin{array}{l}\text{Ammonites} \\ \text{Moab}\end{array}\right.$

Judah

Tyre and Edom are probably grouped together in this stage because in the immediate postexilic period they represented Judah's most vehement mercantile competitors.[39]

The warrant for prophecy by Amos in 3:3–8 is clearly parallel to that of Jeremiah 23:9–23:

> For who has stood in the council of the LORD
> so as to see and to hear his word?
> Who has given heed to his word so as to proclaim it? . . .
> But if they had stood in my council,
> then they would have proclaimed my words to my people,
> and they would have turned them from their evil way,
> and from the evil of their doings.
> Am I a God nearby, says the LORD, and not a God far off?
> (Jer 23:18, 22–23)

The argument in both cases is that the "true prophet" (Amos, Jeremiah) is one dispatched by YHWH, even against the prophet's own decision. Thus the traditions of Amos and Jeremiah present a

---

[39] Ibid., 113.

common claim about how and why it is that harsh prophetic declaration about public issues is authorized; they articulate, moreover, the enormous hazard of dismissing the prophetic word, as is the characteristic propensity of established order, as in the case of Amaziah for Amos (Amos 7:10–17) and Jehoiakim for Jeremiah (Jer 36:20–26). This "theology of the word," shared by the prophetic traditions, makes clear that the word of the prophet is not as easily vetoed as opponents of prophetic truth regularly imagined.

In sum, we see reflected in the small corpus of the twelve minor prophets themes decisive for Jeremiah:

- in Hosea, the pathos of a covenant that permits newness;
- in Obadiah, the rule of YHWH over the nations;
- in Jonah, the freedom for the future given in a theology of repentance; and
- in Amos, the origin and theology of prophetic speech.

On all these counts, the Jeremian tradition stands at the center of the larger prophetic tradition. The articulation of that common tradition in Jeremiah is particularly intense, given the acute public crisis that is the matrix for the dynamism of the tradition of Jeremiah.

JEREMIAH AND THE WRITINGS

There are seven scrolls in the third canon of the Hebrew Bible, the Writings, that in one way or another are connected with the Book of Jeremiah.[40] As will be seen, the relationships among the

---

[40]Generally on the third canon, see Donn F. Morgan, *Between Text and Community: The "Writings" in Canonical Interpretation* (Minneapolis: Fortress, 1990).

traditions are complex and quite variegated. As a consequence, we may only note the interplay in order to understand that the Book of Jeremiah is indeed deeply situated in the ongoing literary, liturgical, and artistic life of Israel.

Jeremiah and the Book of Psalms

Jeremiah delivered a powerful polemic against the Jerusalem temple and in general stood against the ideology of the temple wherein YHWH is made patron of the city, the dynasty, and the urban establishment. The Psalms are likely a reflection of the claims of the Jerusalem temple – perhaps from an earlier period, certainly in the Persian period. Having noticed the prophetic polemic against the temple and the locus of the Psalter in the temple, it is nonetheless evident that Jeremiah is familiar with and readily trades upon the Psalter, the great product of temple liturgy.[41] It is clear that Jeremiah is informed by the cadences, genres, and parlance of the Psalter, even though Jeremiah's use of the Psalms may be seen as quite distinctive in his own context.

The most important study of the relationship of Jeremiah to the Psalter is by Walter Baumgartner, who explored the relationship of the "Lamentations of Jeremiah" to the lament psalms in the Book of Psalms:

> The relationship of Jeremiah's songs of lament to the Psalms is thus considerably more complex than appeared from earlier attempts at a solution. In the main, precisely the oldest view, the one least clouded

---

[41] Two qualifiers to this judgment may be noted, but neither tells against this conclusion. First, the formation of the Psalter is perhaps to be dated to the Persian period, so that it is possible that appeals to particular psalms by the prophet did not necessarily link directly to the temple. Second, Jeremiah's appeal to the Psalter concerns especially the lament psalms, which are the psalms least likely to be linked directly to temple ideology.

by criticism, "namely" that Jeremiah is dependent on the Psalms, has turned out to be correct. In no way – this must be expressly stated – does this mean a victory of traditionalism over criticism.[42]

Instead of citing specific texts that correlate verses in Jeremiah with verses in the Psalter, Baumgartner pays primary attention to the genre of lament psalms that is taken up by Jeremiah and used in the prophetic tradition in particular and quite individual ways. Baumgartner first traces the shape of the genre in the Psalter, a view that has become commonplace since Gunkel.[43] Baumgartner notes the elements of the genre: complaint, petition, motivation (which he calls "motifs"), assurance of being heard, vows, and thanksgiving. On the basis of this analysis, Baumgartner is able to show that Jeremiah makes imaginative use of the genre, a use only possible because Jeremiah had been nurtured in and shaped by such long-established communal cadences. Thus, for example, the lamentation in Jeremiah 15:15–21 clearly exhibits the standard genre.[44] The prophet speaks in verses 15–17; after the *address* in verse 15a, the next lines articulate a *petition* in five imperatives: "remember, visit, bring down, do not take away, know." This is followed in verses 16–17 by *motivations* designed to move YHWH to act. In verse 16, Jeremiah delighted in YHWH's words; in verse 17, Jeremiah is isolated because of his loyalty to YHWH. Verse 18 provides a *complaint* designed to impress YHWH with a depth of need and suffering. First, the speaker declares his increasing pain

---

[42] Walter Baumgartner, *Jeremiah's Poems of Lament* (Sheffield: Almond, 1988), 101.

[43] Ibid., 19–40. On the genre, see Erhard Gerstenberger, "Psalms," in *Old Testament Form Criticism*, ed. John H. Hayes (San Antonio, TX: Trinity University Press, 1974), 200–5; and Hermann Gunkel, *An Introduction to the Psalms*, trans. James D. Nogalski (Macon, GA: Mercer University Press, 1998), 112–98.

[44] Baumgartner, *Jeremiah's Poems of Lament*, 46–51.

and incurable wound. But then, at the end of verse 18, the speaker accuses YHWH of deceit and unreliability. All of these motifs probably belong to the genre of lament.

The psalms of lament characteristically receive a divine response.[45] In Jeremiah 15, that response is given in verses 19–21 (cf. 12:5–6). Whereas the divine response to the lament is typically one of comfort and assurance, here it is initially a tough, demanding summons back to the prophetic task:

> So to begin with Yahweh promises him nothing, except that he may continue to exercise his prophetic office. This service, which brings him so much pain, he "may" continue with! His profession, with all its sorrows, is still his most cherished privilege! There is one condition, it is true: the mouth that proclaims the divine words must not, alongside what is "precious," also utter the "worthless," human laments and petitions![46]

There is, in verses 20–21, a positive assurance given by YHWH, but even that seems guarded and limited:

> There does then follow an eventual promise (vv. 20f.), which should at least make his service a little easier: "You will not be defeated by your enemies, even should the whole nation assail you; for I am with you." But the promise relates only to this one, albeit most important, point, that Yahweh will not let him down. The other matters he has complained about are not answered at all: the deity has no ear for his pains and petitions; nothing is going to change there! Jeremiah now realizes that the way of the prophet means giving up all earthly happiness; he has to be content with that one certainty. The result is similar to that in 12.6; as there, renunciation of joy and happiness.[47]

---

[45] See Patrick D. Miller, *They Cried to the Lord: The Form and Theology of Biblical Prayer* (Minneapolis: Fortress, 1994), 135–77.

[46] Baumgartner, *Jeremiah's Poems of Lament*, 50.

[47] Ibid., 51.

The final lament in Jeremiah 20:7–13 again utilizes the genre.[48] This lament begins in verse 7 with a harsh accusation against YHWH. The term rendered "entice" can also be read as "rape," thus suggesting that YHWH has violated the prophet by dispatching him to an impossible prophetic task. The complaint of verses 8–9 indicates the burden of the prophetic task. The poem abruptly changes course in verse 11 with a statement of trust in YHWH. Verse 12 issues one more petition that YHWH should enact retribution against the enemies of the prophet. Verse 13 issues a Song of Thanksgiving to YHWH, now in a mood of confidence and resolve:

> This verse is often deleted, but hardly with justification. That its "characteristically psalmic tone" cannot be admitted as an argument against authenticity should be evident from our whole discussion. Nor can much significance be attached to the fact that Jeremiah never actually escapes from persecution and shameful treatment (Duhm). For it is an *anticipatory* celebration, expressed in the midst of misery and distress, the fruit of hope and longing, and thus perfectly possible even for Jeremiah. And the most that the mention of "the poor man" tells us is that there may already have existed at that time "poor-man songs" of the type we find in the Psalter.[49]

These two examples from Jeremiah 15:15–21 and 20:7–13, reflective of Baumgartner's work, indicate the way in which the prophetic tradition relies on and makes use of the deep liturgical practice of the temple.[50] To be sure, these uses are extended according to personal passion reflecting the deeply disputatious tone of the Book of Jeremiah. The prophet turns to YHWH because his prophetic

[48] Ibid., comments only on verses 10–13.

[49] Ibid., 62.

[50] Fredrik Lindström, in his *Suffering and Sin: Interpretations of Illness in the Individual Complaint Psalms*, ConBOT 37 (Stockholm: Almqvist and Wiksells, 1994), has most fully made the case for a temple venue for the Psalms that are closest to the Lamentations of Jeremiah.

vocation has placed him in contradiction with most of his contemporaries.

This initial study of Baumgartner is essential for observing the way in which the prophetic tradition counts on the Psalter. Since the time of Baumgartner, of course, scholarship has moved on concerning these same poems. A. R. Diamond, Kathleen M. O'Connor, and Mark S. Smith have shown how the lamentations of Jeremiah function within the Book of Jeremiah to serve the larger purposes of the book.[51] That important canonical perspective, however, depends on the close genre analysis of which Baumgartner is representative.

We may add two details to this appreciation of the utilization of genre. First, while Baumgartner eschews specific quotations, it is worth noting that in Jeremiah 9:1–2 there is a close parallel to Psalm 55:6–8. The relationship between the two texts is of peculiar interest because of the imaginative repositioning of the text in the prophetic tradition. In Psalm 55, the speaker is a characteristic Israelite suppliant. In Jeremiah 9, however, the words of grief have been transposed to the lips of Yhwh, who now becomes the quintessential griever concerning Jeremiah's terminal illness.[52] While the prophetic tradition relies on the Psalter, it does so with astonishing artistic freedom.

Second, while Baumgartner's analysis focuses on laments, the prophetic tradition can of course employ a variety of psalmic genres. Here I call attention to the doxological tradition used in

---

[51] A. R. Diamond, *The Confessions of Jeremiah in Context: Scenes of Prophetic Drama*, JSOTSup 47 (Sheffield: Sheffield Academic Press, 1987); Kathleen M. O'Connor, *The Confessions of Jeremiah: Their Interpretation and Their Role in Chapters 1–25*, SBLDS 94 (Atlanta: Scholars Press, 1987); and Mark S. Smith, *The Laments of Jeremiah and Their Contexts: A Literary and Redactional Study of Jeremiah 11–20*, SBLMS 42 (Atlanta: Scholars Press, 1990).

[52] See Heschel, *The Prophets*, 119–22.

Jeremiah 10:12–13 and the quotation of that text in Jeremiah 51:15–16 (see also 27:5). All of these statements articulate YHWH in wondrous power, in a way not unlike the great hymns of the Psalter as in Psalms 104:2–9; 145:13–20; and 146:5–9. The style of hymnic affirmation is variously adjusted in specific contexts for particular purposes, but the doxological tradition functions to establish YHWH as the key agent in the life of the world. Such doxology that celebrates divine power is a counterpart to the laments that raise a need precisely for such sustaining divine power. The tradition of Jeremiah characteristically undermines the uncritical complacency of Jerusalem – in both complaint and doxology. The prophetic tradition is drawn artistically, but with remarkable imaginative freedom, from the old, deep reservoir of the Psalter. As a consequence, the texts making the high claims for Jerusalem are used to mount a critique of those very claims.

Jeremiah and the Book of Job

Baumgartner's accent on genres in the Book of Jeremiah that reflect the dominant genres of the Psalter provide an appropriate move toward the Book of Job and the relationship of the Jeremian tradition to the Book of Job. Critical questions about the Book of Job are notoriously difficult, so any judgment about the relationship between the two books must be provisional. Nonetheless, the connection between Jeremiah 20:14–18 and Job 3 warrants consideration.

Jeremiah 20:14–18 is placed after 20:7–13 and seems to be the culmination of the laments of Jeremiah.[53] These verses show us

---

[53] See Jack R. Lundbom, *Jeremiah 1–20: A New Translation with Introduction and Commentary*, AB 21 A (New York: Doubleday, 1999), 867.

"Jeremiah at the end of his resources."[54] They constitute an extreme statement of despair, the voice of one abandoned and without a future. Our interest is in the connection between this unit of poetry and the long poem of curse in Job 3:1–26 that begins Job's long dispute with his friends and with God. The relationship between the two passages is not clear, though the probability is that the Job complaint is derivative of that of Jeremiah. John Bright, in commenting on Jeremiah 20:14–18, concludes:

> One can neither exaggerate the agony of spirit revealed here, nor improve on the words which Jeremiah found to express it. There is, indeed, little in all of literature that compares with this piece, and nothing in the Bible except perhaps the third chapter of Job, to which it is very similar. Whether Job develops the thought of this passage or whether both derive from a common tradition is a question that cannot be answered with assurance; but kinship between the two is undeniable.[55]

Whatever the case, we may at least entertain the possibility that the historical vocation of Jeremiah gives rise in Israel to the fictional character of Job, or that Job is the character of Jeremiah writ large and in extremis, even though the Book of Job has other non-Israelite antecedents. The connection between the two passages, both of which articulate acute alienation from God and from the human community, invites a reflection on the more general connection between Jeremiah and Job and the world of crisis that they occupy together. Claus Westermann has provided an acute analysis of the genre of the Book of Job and has shown that the lament is

[54] John Bright, *Jeremiah: Translated with an Introduction and Notes*, AB 21 (Garden City, NY: Doubleday, 1965), 134.
[55] Ibid.

the dominant genre of the book.[56] Westermann observes that the lament of Job begins in the disputed chapter 3 and concludes with the disputatious speeches of chapters 29–31.

It is not necessary to imagine that the lament pattern in Job derives from Jeremiah, as there are ample resources elsewhere. It is nonetheless useful to notice that the same triad of concerns is voiced in Jeremiah:

1. The *"Self-lament"* in Jeremiah is poignant in his "Lamentations."[57] Thus, for example, in Jeremiah 15:16–17, Jeremiah exhibits profound self-pity:

> Your words were found, and I ate them,
> and your words became to me a joy
> and the delight of my heart;
> for I am called by your name,
> O LORD, God of hosts.
> I did not sit in the company of merrymakers,
> nor did I rejoice;
> under the weight of your hand I sat alone,
> for you had filled me with indignation. (Jer 15:16–17)

2. The *lament about enemies* is appropriate because Jeremiah is clearly under assault from other members of his community.[58] Thus he accuses the "men of Anathoth" (11:21) and mentions his "persecutors" (15:15; 17:18), his "adversaries" (18:19), and his betrayal by his friends (20:10).

---

[56] See Claus Westermann, *The Structure of the Book of Job: A Form-Critical Analysis* (Philadelphia: Fortress, 1981), 31: "The lament comprises by far the most prevalent formal element in the Book of Job." Westermann lists the several laments that occur in the speeches of Job.

[57] Ibid., 46–50.

[58] Ibid., 43–46.

3. The *accusation against God* is voiced by Jeremiah as he accuses YHWH of being "a deceitful brook" (15:18), a political "terror to me" (17:17), and one who has "seduced" him into a prophetic vocation (20:7).[59] On all counts Jeremiah is, in his prophetic function, as beleaguered as Job. And Jeremiah's voice is every bit as shrill, disputatious, and demanding as Job's.

In his analysis of the genre of the Book of Job, Westermann observed Job's assertion of innocence and his avowal of trust (Job 7). In this connection, it is worth recalling the praise of God that is typically the culmination of such lament structures.[60] In the tradition of Jeremiah, we have noticed the doxology of Jeremiah 10:1–16 and should pay particular attention to 20:13, which in one sense is the culmination of all of the lamentations:

> Sing to the LORD;
> praise the LORD!
> For he has delivered the life of the needy
> from the hands of evildoers. (Jer 20:13)

Beyond that, we might wonder if the Oracles Against the Nations in Jeremiah 46–51 should be taken as a counterpoint to doxology. In the whirlwind speeches of Job (Job 38–41), the creator engages in self-praise for being the supreme governor of all creation, capable of ruling the monsters (Behemoth and Leviathan) in an orderly and splendid way. Although the Oracles Against the Nations in Jeremiah are much more shrill, in the end they also celebrate the sovereignty of YHWH, who will defeat every recalcitrant vassal state. As the Oracles Against the Nations report the complete domination of YHWH, so they function to position Jeremiah among the nations as Job is positioned among the monsters. In the end, recalcitrant

---

[59] Ibid., 30–59.
[60] Ibid., 73, 77.

Job, recalcitrant Babylon, and even self-pitying Jeremiah perforce come to terms with the rule of Yʜwʜ, who plucks up and tears down but also plants and builds.

Again, it is not possible to determine how directly Job is informed by or derivative of Jeremiah if at all. But there are still important heuristic gains in the juxtaposition of the two texts. It is clear that both texts utilize the same genres of lament and doxology. It is also clear that both utilize these genres in order to enter the contested world of the righteous sufferer. In the case of Job and the sapiential antecedents of Job, the "righteous sufferer" is "everyman" (that is, every person), who must live in a cold world where the gods may be triumphant but scarcely responsive. In the case of Jeremiah, we are able to see that the theme of the righteous sufferer pertains quintessentially to the prophetic vocation. It is his "call" that has made Jeremiah an alienated self, placed him in dispute with his fellows, and set him before a God who "entices." The prophetic vocation, the "everyman" of righteous suffering writ large, is a compelling vehicle for voicing the unbearable contradiction between divine governance and the human (in this case, Israelite) propensity for self-deception and distorted autonomy. The contradiction itself is nearly unimaginable.

The only truth more acute is that *the contradiction must be uttered.* When spoken, it sounds like treason (Jer 38:4) and leads to hostility (Jer 26:11). But it must be spoken. It is for that reason that this prophet arrives at "well-nigh suicidal despair."[61] The drama of Job draws a wide exposé of such righteous suffering. It also seems plausible that in Israel the drama of Job emerges in the unbearable world of contradiction so deeply lived by Jeremiah and so well uttered by Jeremiah.

[61] Bright, *Jeremiah*, 134.

Jeremiah and the Book of Proverbs

There is no convincing ground from which to hypothesize any significant relationship between the Book of Jeremiah and the Book of Proverbs. But with the connections to the Book of Job noted earlier, we are entitled to inquire about the possible relationship of Jeremiah to the tradition of wisdom teaching in general, of which the Book of Proverbs is the clearest example.[62] We may identify a number of dimensions to the question, the answers to which indicate that the Book of Jeremiah did know about and to some extent appealed to the wisdom traditions, as long as "wisdom tradition" is understood as the deposit of critical empirical reflection on the divine ordering of creation that ensures moral coherence and a trustworthy connection between choices (deeds) and consequences. The wisdom teachers, reflecting a creation theology, attest to the hidden ways of YHWH's governance of the world that is to be detected by attending to the recurring patterns of conduct and consequences.[63]

First, it is plausible that there were highly visible "wisdom teachers" who were known to have particular gifts of discernment but who were excessively accommodating to the status quo and who were, inevitably, opponents of Jeremiah. Such an adversarial social reality is likely suggested by Jeremiah 8:8–9 and 18:18. The instruction of 9:23–24 is also pertinent insofar as it reprimands those who have excessive confidence and pride in their capacity to discern

---

[62] Behind the connection between Jeremiah and wisdom may be the connection between the Book of Deuteronomy and wisdom. On the latter, see Moshe Weinfeld, *Deuteronomy and the Deuteronomic School* (Oxford: Clarendon, 1972).

[63] On this pattern, see Klaus Koch, "Is There a Doctrine of Retribution in the Old Testament?" in *Theodicy in the Old Testament*, ed. James L. Crenshaw, IRT 4 (Philadelphia: Fortress, 1983), 57–87.

the hidden connections of social reality. The tradition of Jeremiah rejects such teaching.

Second, however, it is apparent that Jeremiah is alert to proverbial sayings and can readily employ them for his own purposes.[64] Consider the following examples:

> Even the stork in the heavens
> knows its times;
> and the turtledove, swallow, and crane
> observe the time of their coming;
> but my people do not know
> the ordinance of the LORD. (Jer 8:7)

You shall speak to them this word: Thus says the LORD, the God of Israel: Every wine-jar should be filled with wine. And they will say to you, "Do you think we do not know that every wine-jar should be filled with wine?" (Jer 13:12)

Can iron and bronze break iron from the north? (Jer 15:12)

* * *

> Does the snow of Lebanon leave
> the crags of Sirion?
> Do the mountain waters run dry,
> the cold flowing streams? (Jer 18:14)

Let the prophet who has a dream tell the dream, but let the one who has my word speak my word faithfully. What has straw in common with wheat? says the LORD. (Jer 23:28)

> In those days they shall no longer say:
> "The parents have eaten sour grapes,
> and the children's teeth are set on edge." (Jer 31:29)

[64] See Johannes Lindblom, "Wisdom in the Old Testament Prophets," in *Wisdom in Israel and in the Ancient Near East*, ed. M. Noth and D. Winton Thomas, VTSup 3 (Leiden: Brill, 1955), 192–204.

In addition to these proverbial sayings that may have been quite popular, Jeremiah 10:23–25 presents a teaching not unlike some Proverbs concerning the hidden capacity of YHWH to overrule the "connection" of deed and consequence:

> I know, O LORD, that the way of
> human beings is not in their control,
> that mortals as they walk
> cannot direct their steps. (Jer 10:23)

Gerhard von Rad identified six teachings in the Book of Proverbs that are parallel to this one in Jeremiah.[65] These statements affirm that, in the end, human discernment, and therefore human conduct, must yield to divine mystery.

In Jeremiah 17:5–11, Jack R. Lundbom has observed the pragmatic dimension of wisdom reflection that is quite parallel to the Book of Proverbs.[66] In 17:5–8, in a teaching that closely parallels Psalm 1, the text traces out "the two ways" of "blessing and curse" that govern wisdom teaching. The curse comes on those who live as though autonomous; the blessing is given to those who eschew such autonomy and trust in YHWH. Verses 9–10 affirm the way in which YHWH probes human intentionality and examines hidden motives. This theme is common in wisdom teaching, but see also Jeremiah 6:27–30.

Third, we may particularly note the use of the term *mûsār*, variously rendered "correction, discipline, punishment, or nurture."[67] The several uses of the term in Jeremiah suggest that one (Israel)

---

[65] Gerhard von Rad, *Old Testament Theology I* (San Francisco: Harper and Row, 1962), 439.

[66] Lundbom, *Jeremiah*, 779–92.

[67] See Hans-Joachim Kraus, "Geschichte als Erziehung," in *Probleme biblischer Theologie: Gerhard von Rad zum 70. Geburtstag*, ed. Hans Walter Wolff (Munich: Kaiser, 1971), 258–74.

can be inculcated into a tradition of responsibility in the way a child is nurtured into family norms. Indeed, this is exactly the work of wisdom instruction. For the most part, it is asserted that Israel, in its waywardness, has refused such nurture and discipline in its stubborn autonomy (see Jer 2:30; 5:3; 7:28; 17:23; 32:33; 35:13). But the norms are intractable, and so such waywardness inescapably evokes punishment (see Jer 2:19; 30:14; 31:18). Only in the end, in a promise of new beginning, does Israel reverse itself and accept the discipline that makes newness possible:

> Indeed I heard Ephraim pleading:
> "You disciplined me, and I took the *discipline* [*wā'iwwāsēr*]
> I was like a calf untrained.
> Bring me back, let me come back,
> for you are the LORD my God." (Jer 31:18)

The use of the root *ysr* (whence come both *mûsār* and *wā'iwwāsēr*) surely suggests that the Jeremian tradition understood very well the slow work of nurture and the destructive implications of refusing such nurture. It is clear that the prophet uses such a notion of pedagogical nurture primarily to bespeak a threat on the endangered city. Because Jer 31:18 is located in the promissory materials, we may take it to mean that only after the judgment is Israel prepared to take discipline and so "come back." The significance of this usage is that the prophet insists that sapiential traditions of discipline cannot be circumvented.

Fourth, in two doxological passages, a hymnic voice credits wisdom as a property or agency through which YHWH has created the world:

> It is he who made the earth by his power,
> who established the world by his wisdom,
> and by his understanding stretched out the heavens.
> (Jer 10:12; see also 51:15)

These passages suggest the sapiential conviction that Yhwh's creation is shot through with moral coherence and divine intentionality that are intrinsic to creation itself. Although no direct appeal is made here to Proverbs 8:22–31, the two doxological statements in Jeremiah bespeak the world of that famous text. In Proverbs 8, wisdom declares itself to be an aide to the creator in the forming and governing of the world, in guaranteeing that the world is open toward life. In these two texts in Jeremiah, it is clear that the wise God of creation is contrasted with the foolishness of the idols that can only produce death.

Together these scattered and fragmentary data attest that the prophetic tradition drew easily and frequently on the wisdom traditions reflected in the Book of Proverbs. This means that even while the prophet is bent on asserting discontinuity in Jerusalem, at the same time there is serious reflection on and engagement with the abiding continuities that make a life of well-being possible. This conviction indicates the breadth of the interpretive world that the prophet inhabited.

Jeremiah and the Book of Lamentations

The Book of Lamentations comprises five poems (four of which are acrostics) that grieve the destruction of Jerusalem.[68] It is most credible to assume that the poems emerged soon after the razing of the city in 587 BCE; that is, well within the lifetime of Jeremiah. There is no doubt that Jeremiah had looked the destruction of Jerusalem full in the face and knew about the dismay and consternation that

---

[68] For recent studies of the Book of Lamentations, see Kathleen M. O'Connor, *Lamentations and the Tears of the World* (Maryknoll, NY: Orbis, 2002); Tod Linafelt, *Surviving Lamentations: Catastrophe, Lament, and Protest in the Afterlife of a Biblical Book* (Chicago: University of Chicago Press, 2000); and Nancy C. Lee, *The Singers of Lamentations: Cities under Siege, from Ur to Jerusalem to Sarajevo*, BIS 60 (Leiden: Brill, 2002).

the destruction would cause. Thus, a link between Lamentations and Jeremiah is popular and traditional, not least because Jeremiah, as we have seen, articulates his own lamentations.

The link between Jeremiah and Lamentations is based on two pieces of textual evidence beyond the general pattern of lament.[69] First, the LXX, and derivatively the Vulgate, has prefaced the beginning of the poetry with a suggestive superscription:

> Before 1:1 of MT, the LXX has this preface: "And it came to pass after Israel had been taken captive and Jerusalem had been laid waste, Jeremiah sat weeping and lamented this lament over Jerusalem, and said . . . " The Vulgate also contains this prologue, in nearly identical form. Though this is a later addition to the text, based on the identification of Jeremiah as author of the book, note that the style is Hebraic rather than Greek. Either it was translated from a Hebrew *Vorlage*, or the author imitated the style of biblical Greek.[70]

This superscription in the Greek has been replicated in various forms in the Latin, the Aramaic, and the Syriac to provide a popular notion of Jeremiah's authorship of Lamentations. It must be underscored, however, that in the Hebrew text itself there is no such reference to Jeremiah, so that the connection of Lamentations to Jeremiah is generally thought to be a later development in the tradition.

Second, 2 Chronicles 35:25, a late text from the Persian period, ascribes laments to Jeremiah:

> Jeremiah also uttered a lament for Josiah, and all the singing men and singing women have spoken of Josiah in their laments to this day. They made these a custom in Israel; they are recorded in the Laments. (2 Chr 35:25)

---

[69] Delbert R. Hillers, *Lamentations: A New Translation with Introduction and Commentary*, AB 7A (Garden City, NY: Doubleday, 1972), xix–xxiii.

[70] Ibid., 5.

This reference, however, has no connection with the Book of Lamentations. It refers, rather, to the death of the good king Josiah, to whom the prophet Jeremiah had paid attention in Jeremiah 22:15–16, even though in that passage the grief expressed refers to Jehoiakim and not to Josiah (see 22:18–19).

On both these counts, a direct connection between the Book of Lamentations and Jeremiah is not persuasive. That the themes of the Book of Lamentations follow from the oracles of Jeremiah makes sense, so that the two live in the same "intellectual world" of loss and grief. Beyond that, however, no notion of authorship of the Book of Lamentations by Jeremiah is taken to be credible in current critical discussion.

Jeremiah and the Book of Chronicles

The Book of Chronicles is a Persian document concerning the long history of monarchal Judah. Its two parts offer a different vision of the royal history from the Book of Kings. Because they are dated in the Persian period, they not only pay acute attention to the final failure of Jerusalem (see 2 Chr 36:5–21) but also look beyond the judgment and deportation to the return of exiles and the restoration of Jerusalem (see 2 Chr 36:22–23). These verses from 2 Chronicles 36 are of peculiar interest because they constitute the very final verses of the Hebrew Bible, a text that thus culminates with an anticipation of restoration in Jerusalem.

It is clear that the Chronicler's material is long after the person of Jeremiah, and perhaps after the compilation of the final form of the Book of Jeremiah, though the latter is not certain. In any case, we are astonished to find in 2 Chronicles 35–36 four references to the prophet Jeremiah. These references serve to indicate that the tradition of Jeremiah continued to be a lively source of faith and interpretation well into the Persian period. It is more than a little odd that Jeremiah is never mentioned in the Book of Kings. But now, in the later text of Chronicles, Jeremiah is taken to be a primary interpreter and primary anticipation of what Yhwh yet has in store for the community of Israel.

First, in 2 Chronicles 35:25, Jeremiah is among those who lament the violent death of Josiah. Whatever may be made of such a notation historically, it comes as no surprise that the prophet should lament this particular king (see Jer 22:15–16). Josiah is the quintessential king of the Torah tradition of the Deuteronomist who perfectly keeps the Torah and models the way in which power serves the Torah. Josiah's death, in such purview, amounts to a defeat of the Torah traditions and, consequently, a huge step toward the destruction of the city (see 2 Kings 23:25–27). So, in grieving the fallen king, the prophet grieves the defeat of the entire "Torah-option" for Jerusalem he had so long championed. There were other kings yet to reign in Jerusalem after Josiah (see 2 Kings 23:31–25:7), but for Jeremiah and for the Deuteronomistic historian, the death of Josiah meant the end of an alternative possibility. In this light, 2 Chronicles 35:25 is about grief over a particular theological advocacy.

Second, in 2 Chronicles 36:12, Jeremiah is cited as the one who had urged King Zedekiah away from his foolish policies, advocating instead a peaceable submission to Nebuchadnezzar. This judgment on Zedekiah, reflecting the geopolitical projection of the Jeremian tradition, is amply attested in the Book of Jeremiah (see Jer 21:3–7; 27:12–15; 37:1–10; 38:14–28). The citation of the prophet in 2 Chronicles 36 conforms to what we know about the prophet and his engagement with an unresponsive monarchy.

Third, in 2 Chronicles 36:17–21, the "king of the Chaldeans" operates, as the prophet had said, to effect divine judgment on Jerusalem. We have already seen that Nebuchadnezzar is regarded by the prophet as a vehicle of divine judgment (see Jer 25:9; 27:6). In 2 Chronicles 36:21, the particular reference to the prophet alludes especially to Jeremiah 25:12 and 29:10, wherein the tradition of Jeremiah moves toward apocalyptic rhetoric and begins to attach a timetable to the issues of judgment and restoration that preoccupied the tradition:

> This whole land shall become a ruin and a waste, and these nations shall serve the king of Babylon seventy years. Then *after seventy years* are completed, I will punish the king of Babylon and that nation, the land of the Chaldeans, for their iniquity, says the LORD, making the land an everlasting waste. (Jer 25:11–12)

> For thus says the LORD: Only when Babylon's *seventy years* are completed will I visit you, and I will fulfill to you my promise and bring you back to this place. (Jer 29:10)

The numbers are (and become) a symbolic way of speaking and should not be taken literally. What matters here is that 2 Chronicles 36:21 takes up the reference from Jeremiah and utilizes it to assert, consistent with Jeremiah, that the time for punishment of Jerusalem is over.

Fourth, of the four references to Jeremiah in 2 Chronicles, the final one in 2 Chronicles 36:22 is most remarkable and surely the most important:

> In the first year of King Cyrus of Persia, in fulfillment of the word of the LORD spoken by Jeremiah, the LORD stirred up the spirit of King Cyrus of Persia so that he sent a herald throughout all his kingdom and also declared in a written edict. (2 Chr 36:22)

In these very last verses of the Hebrew Bible, Jeremiah is cited as the one who promised that YHWH would "stir up" (*hēʿîr* from ʿwr) Cyrus, for it is Cyrus the Persian who terminates Babylonian hegemony and who will permit the Jews to return home (see Isa 41:2; 44:28; 45:1; as well as the parallel in Ezra 1:1–4).

When we probe the Jeremian tradition to locate the word quoted here, it is most likely that the verses in the final oracle against Babylon provide the basis for this citation:

> For I am going to *stir up* [*mēʿîr*] and bring against Babylon a company of great nations from the land of the north; and they shall array themselves against her; from there she shall be taken. Their arrows are like the arrows of a skilled warrior who does not return empty-handed. (Jer 50:9; see also 50:45–46; 51:1)

> Sharpen the arrows!
> Fill the quivers!

> The LORD has *stirred up* [*hēʿîr*] the spirit of the kings of the Medes, because his purpose concerning Babylon is to destroy it, for that is the vengeance of the LORD, vengeance for his temple. (Jer 51:11)

The verb "stir up" (ʿwr) is an appropriately elusive one that does not specify how the hidden impetus of YHWH operates. The agent to be "stirred up," moreover, is left unnamed in Jeremiah but is now supplied by Chronicles as in Isaiah 44:45. Thus the "fulfillment" of the prophetic word of Jeremiah in Cyrus is only fulfillment because the interpreting community has cited the relevant promise that is, by an act of the imagination, drawn into connection with the contemporary rise of Persia. By making this connection, Jeremiah – whose anticipations for restored Jerusalem are vague and elusive – becomes the one through whom YHWH has designated Cyrus as an agent of divine restoration. Thus, in his articulation of grief (2 Chr 35:25), judgment (2 Chr 36:2, 21), and hope (2 Chr 36:22–23), Jeremiah is taken to be the true voice of YHWH concerning the destiny of Israel and the future of Judaism.

In utilizing the Jeremian tradition in this way, we remain very close to the governing verbs of Jeremiah 1:10. Jeremiah is the authorizer of both plucking up and tearing down and building and planting. The Hebrew Bible ends on "building and planting" made historically possible by Cyrus but made theologically credible by Jeremiah.

Jeremiah and the Book of Ezra

The Book of Ezra begins in 1:1–5 with the same references to Jeremiah that we have seen in 2 Chronicles 36:22–23. The repetition provides continuity in the literature and connects the narrative of Ezra to the return of exiled Jews anticipated in 2 Chronicles 36:22–23. The reference to Jeremiah is the only explicit connection between the Book of Ezra and Jeremiah, and one may conclude that it is a secondary editorial maneuver.

But, beyond this one explicit reference, we may notice a less direct but more substantive connection, "namely," the movement in the Book of Jeremiah *from the prophetic to the scribal*.[71] In the end, it is Baruch who dominates the Book of Jeremiah, along with his brother scribe Seriah (see Jer 36, 43, 45, 51). The movement toward scribalism in emerging Judaism culminates in Ezra, "a scribe skilled in the Torah of Moses that the LORD God of Israel had given" (Ezra 7:6). Thus we may hypothesize that the final form of the Book of Jeremiah, in its scribal attenuation, is one of the accomplishments of later scribalism that became dominant in emerging Judaism.

---

[71] On the cruciality of the scribe, see James Muilenburg, "Baruch the Scribe," in *A Prophet to the Nations: Essays in Jeremiah Studies*, ed. Leo G. Perdue and Brian W. Kovacs (Winona Lake, IN: Eisenbrauns, 1984), 229–45; and the more recent, somewhat polemical, discussion by Philip R. Davies, *Scribes and Schools: Canonization of the Hebrew Scriptures*, LAI (Louisville, KY: Westminster John Knox, 1998).

Jeremiah and the Book of Daniel

The Book of Daniel constitutes the primary apocalyptic statement of the Old Testament, a mode of literature in the faith that anticipates a cataclysmic upheaval in the public world of kingdoms and empires. The Book of Daniel has before it a great statement of world history and the successive rise and fall of many kingdoms. For our purposes, it is not necessary to review the complex and awesome picture traced by the text. It is enough for us to recognize that in the late developments of the Book of Jeremiah, particularly in chapter 25, Jeremiah opens toward apocalyptic thinking and anticipates a great world upheaval caused by God. We have already noticed in that connection the use of the verb "stir up" (*'wr*), the verb also used in 2 Chronicles 36:22, as a signal for great upheavals in world history.

Daniel 9 purposes a great time of world events under Darius the Persian. Of interest here is verse 2, with its direct allusion to Jeremiah. As we have seen, the developed tradition of Jeremiah, well beyond the prophet himself, has fixed the time of deportation for Jerusalem at seventy years, after which there will be a restoration (see Jer 25:11–12; 29:10). This reference in Jeremiah, scarcely developed at all, in Daniel becomes the grounds for future expectation:

> In the first year of his reign, I, Daniel, perceived in the books the number of years that, according to the word of the LORD to the prophet Jeremiah, must be fulfilled for the devastation of Jerusalem, "namely," *seventy years.* (Dan 9:2)

With that mention of Jeremiah and the number seventy, there follows in Daniel 9 a plan for the future that runs in the direction of apocalyptic numerology (see Dan 9:24–26). This statement is well beyond the horizon of Jeremiah. It is important that by this time the saying of Jeremiah has been transposed from *promise* to *decree*

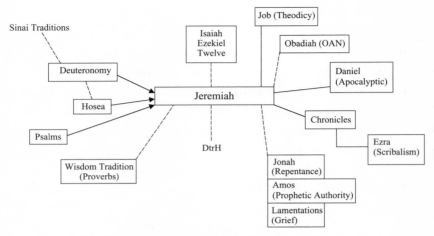

Chart 1. Jeremiah in the midst of Old Testament literature

(*ḥtk*; cf. *ḥrṣ* in vv. 26, 27), now a fixed, settled point in a predetermined future. This mode of reasoning is very different from that of the Jeremian tradition, but it is nonetheless rooted there.

CONCLUSION

This account of the location of Jeremiah within the Old Testament makes clear that the Book of Jeremiah stands pivotally at the center of the Old Testament and occupies a primary position vis-à-vis the decisive crisis of Old Testament faith (see Chart 1).

Jeremiah shares with the other prophetic books – Isaiah, Ezekiel, and the Twelve – the general theme of judgment and restoration. Jeremiah draws on the covenantal traditions of Deuteronomy and Hosea, rooted in Sinai memories, and is sustained by the sapiential materials in the Book of Psalms. The Book of Jeremiah, however, is not only *receptive* to antecedent traditions but also powerfully *generative* for the future of Jewish faith, contributing directly to scribal and apocalyptic traditions and to the ongoing dispute over theodicy. Within this location amid the deep crisis of the loss of Jerusalem, the Book of Jeremiah, by means of its candor about judgment and its buoyancy about restoration, draws the narrative of the incomparable God close to the abyss of discontinuity.[72] It manifests a remarkable imaginative freedom in its utilization of older materials and in its generation of new materials. That imaginative freedom, moreover, is deeply commensurate with the God to whom it wondrously and disputatiously attests.

The tradition of Jeremiah shrewdly holds together an affirmation of *the rule of* Yhwh, the creator over all the world and the peoples and the kingdoms that dwell therein, and *the peculiar status of Israel* as God's intractably beloved people. What distinguishes this prophetic tradition, however, is its rhetorical capacity to descend fully and without reserve *into the abyss of displacement* and to ponder the radical devastation of that in which Israel has long trusted.

This radical discontinuity is glaringly exhibited when it is accompanied – as it characteristically is in the Jeremian tradition – by an affirmation of Yhwh as the God *who makes new and who calls into existence the things that do not exist.* This deep access to both *loss* and *newness* places the Jeremian tradition and its vibrant interpretive stream in deep conflict with the royal and priestly traditions of the Old Testament that seek to maintain the static givenness of life in Israel and the world and that celebrate a God-guaranteed continuity despite all trouble. This interface between traditions of discontinuity and traditions of continuity is perhaps the defining issue in Old Testament theology, an issue that continues to haunt synagogue and church and continues to vex every high culture that

---

[72] See Walter Brueggemann, "Meditation on the Abyss: The Book of Jeremiah," *WW* 22 (2002): 340–50.

thrives on continuity and is willing to engage in denial and brutality in order to fend off the threat of discontinuity. Jeremiah understood that, eventually, discontinuity could not be fended off – if and when it is the will and purpose of the creator to cause an ending and to undo the world (see Jer 4:23–26).

CHAPTER 4

The Continuing Influence of the Book of Jeremiah

The Book of Jeremiah, in its complex, multivocal final form, attests to the reality, liveliness, and decisiveness of the incomparable God in relationship to the defining crisis of Old Testament faith. The book is, in effect, a piercing theological meditation on the abyss of Jerusalem. In that abyss, all traditional and institutional forms of faith were placed in jeopardy. Beyond the abyss, the future is given in new forms and shapes in inscrutable ways by the God who presides over the abyss.[1] But the Book of Jeremiah is not only a reflection on displacement and restoration as lived, historical realities in an ancient city in the sixth century BCE. It is instead vigorous testimony that the will, purpose, and action of the incomparable God of holiness and compassion constitute the decisive clue to the meaning of that crisis. The Book of Jeremiah attests that *loss* in the city is the will of YHWH, who will not be mocked, and that *renewal* in the city is the will of YHWH, who will not abandon either the world YHWH has created and governed or the peculiar people YHWH has rescued and commanded into existence. The Book of Jeremiah is thus quite context-specific.

---

[1] See Walter Brueggemann, "Meditation upon the Abyss: The Book of Jeremiah," *WW* 22 (2002): 340–50.

At the same time, it is clear that the Book of Jeremiah continues to be a generative, credible, and pertinent testimony wherein human persons and human communities face the abyss of disruption and ponder the possibility of post-abyss futures. Such a credible and poignant testimony matters at the turn of the twenty-first century, in which discerning people can notice a world in profound jeopardy not unlike the profound jeopardy of that ancient city of Jerusalem and that beloved people of Israel. But before considering Jeremiah now, we may profit from attention to the use of Jeremiah in the New Testament.

JEREMIAH AND THE NEW TESTAMENT

It is clear that the Book of Jeremiah was a lively force in the early church as it obviously was in the ongoing life of early Judaism. First, it is possible to notice the following four particular allusions to the tradition of Jeremiah that are important to the interpretive practice of the New Testament.[2]

1. In the narrative of Herod's "slaughter of the innocents," Jeremiah 31:15 is quoted:

> A voice was heard in Ramah,
> wailing and loud lamentation,
> Rachel weeping for her children;
> she refused to be consoled,
> because they are no more. (Matt 2:18)

The wholesale slaughter of young babies at the hand of royal power is presented through the grief of mother Rachel, which is, in the

---

[2] See J. W. Mazurel, "Citations from the Book of Jeremiah in the New Testament," in *Reading the Book of Jeremiah: A Search for Coherence*, ed. Martin Kessler (Winona Lake, IN: Eisenbrauns, 2004), 181–89.

tradition, twinned with the grief of father Jacob (see Gen 37:34–35). The Gospel of Matthew appeals to the grief of Israel and the loss of Jerusalem in order to voice the grief of these belated state murders. Emil Fackenheim has shown how this reverence for Rachel's grief lingers in the contemporary world.[3]

2. In Matthew 16:14, in response to the question of Jesus, the disciples report on popular expectation and the images through which the Jesus movement is interpreted:

> And they said, "Some say John the Baptist, but others Elijah, and still others Jeremiah or one of the prophets." (Matt 16:14)

Jeremiah is here twinned with Elijah as one who would "come again." Clearly the tradition has not finished with Jeremiah.

3. In Matthew 21:13, in a condemnation of temple practices, Jesus has combined the phrasing of Jeremiah from Jeremiah 7:11 together with Isaiah 56:7 to state the intention of the temple and its distorted contemporary practice:

> He said to them, "It is written,
> 'My house shall be called a house of prayer';
> but you are making it a den of robbers." (Matt 21:13)

4. Matthew 27:9 reports on the proper disposal of the "blood money" of Judas, who had betrayed Jesus. The money is deployed

---

[3] See Emil Fackenheim, "New Hearts and the Old Covenant: On Some Possibilities of a Fraternal Jewish–Christian Reading of the Jewish Bible Today," in *The Divine Helmsman: Studies on God's Control of Human Events, Presented to Lou H. Silberman*, ed. James L. Crenshaw and Samuel Sandmel (New York: Ktav, 1980), 191–205; and Walter Brueggemann, "Texts That Linger, Words That Explode," *ThTo* 54 (1997): 180–99, reprinted in *Texts that Linger, Words that Explode: Listening to Prophetic Voices*, ed. Patrick D. Miller (Minneapolis: Fortress, 2000), 1–19. Note also Kathleen D. Billman and Daniel L. Migliore, *Rachel's Cry: Prayer of Lament and Rebirth of Hope* (Cleveland, OH: United Church Press, 1999).

in order to purchase a burial place for foreigners. This passage in Matthew is curious, if not confused, because the text quoted in Matthew 27:9–10 is from Zechariah 11:13. Scholars conjecture that the mistaken reference to Jeremiah is based on the awareness that in Jeremiah 32:6–9 (see also Jer 18:1–2), Jeremiah is also commanded by YHWH to buy a field.[4] That the Zechariah citation could be reassigned to Jeremiah attests to the powerful way in which Jeremiah was on the horizon of the Gospel of Matthew. It is also to be noted that the uncertainty of the text is evidence that some text traditions note variously Zechariah and Isaiah. This text in Matthew 27 should not, therefore, count strongly for Jeremiah's influence, except to note the permeation of the Jeremian tradition in such an odd way. Regardless, it is obvious that at key points in Matthew's Gospel, Jeremiah is cited. The sum of such citations may indicate not ad hoc references but an inchoate attempt to narrate the account of Jesus according to the tradition of Jeremiah.[5]

Second, more important than the Matthean texts is the remarkable quotation of Jeremiah 31:31–34 in Hebrews 8:8–12. The letter to the Hebrews presents the Gospel of the early church according to a variety of Old Testament traditions. But it is verse 13 that is important because of its use of the term "obsolete" (*palaioō*). This usage shows how in the Letter to the Hebrews the old claim of the

---

[4] See Floyd Filson, *A Commentary on the Gospel According to Saint Matthew*, Black's New Testament Commentary (London: Adam and Charles Black, 1971), 288; and William F. Albright and C. S. Morris, *Matthew: Introduction, Translation, and Notes*, AB 26 (New York: Doubleday, 1971), 341.

[5] On the way in which New Testament narratives of Jesus replicate extended Old Testament narratives, see David P. Moessner, *Lord of the Banquet: The Literary and Theological Significance of the Lukan Travel Narrative* (Harrisburg, PA: Trinity Press International, 1989); and Thomas L. Brodie, *The Crucial Bridge: The Elijah–Elisha Narrative as an Interpretive Synthesis of Genesis–Kings and a Literary Model for the Gospels* (Collegeville, PA: Liturgical, 2000).

Old Testament is characteristically overcome by its New Testament counterpart. Thus "old covenant–new covenant" is read here in a supersessionist way, so that the text of the Old Testament is used against the Old Testament itself. It is neither necessary nor legitimate to read Jeremiah 31:34 in such a supersessionist way.[6] But the Hebrews text is important because it is a clear example of the way in which the early church, by appeal to Jeremiah, understood the truth of Jesus to displace the truth of Israel.[7] Somewhat ironically, the citation indicates the cruciality of the Jeremian tradition for the church's self-understanding, even if the Jeremian tradition is handled in a supersessionist way.

Third, beyond particular citations, we have pondered at some length that the structural assumption of the Book of Jeremiah (signaled in 1:10) is a twofold movement *into the abyss* and *out of the abyss*. That is, the lived reality of Jerusalem is outlined in Jeremiah and understood both in and out of the abyss as the will of Yhwh (see Jer 31:28). That twofold movement is evident everywhere in the New Testament, as, for example, in the primal Christian hymn of 1 Corinthians 15:3–4: "that Christ died . . . that he was raised on the third day." Thus the theological drama of *displacement and restoration* is readily transposed, in Christian testimony, into *crucifixion and resurrection*. Another counterpart is found in John 2:19–22. The *destruction of the temple* (read: plucking up and tearing down) and the *raising of the temple* (read: building and planting) turn out now to be a reference to "his body" in Christ's death and resurrection.

---

[6] On this text, see Norbert Lohfink, *The Covenant Never Revoked: Biblical Reflections on Christian–Jewish Dialogue* (New York: Paulist, 1991); and Hans Walter Wolff, *Confrontations with Prophets: Discovering the Old Testament's New and Contemporary Significance* (Philadelphia: Fortress, 1983), 49–62.

[7] On pervasive supersessionism in Christian tradition, see R. Kendall Soulen, *The God of Israel and Christian Theology* (Minneapolis: Fortress, 1996).

In this way, the dramatic movement of Jeremiah (more so than anywhere else in the Old Testament) readily becomes the *Friday–Sunday dramatic narrative of the church*.[8] It is clear that Jeremiah's cruciality for New Testament faith consists not in particular citations but in the imaginative redescription of the crisis of Jerusalem according to the large purposes of YHWH.

JEREMIAH NOW

Every Christian preacher, mutatis mutandis, is regularly engaged in the same imaginative rereading of reality through the crisis of Jesus. The church found in the narrative of Jesus the same incomparable God of death and new life so vividly given in the Jeremian tradition. Because the Book of Jeremiah is concerned with descent into the abyss and restoration from the abyss according to the power and fidelity of the incomparable God, the Jeremian text – beyond the New Testament – continues to be a pertinent testimony wherever the human community must ponder durable truth in the face of the abyss. We may consider this interface of durable truth and abyss in three quite different ways.

First, of all of the brutalities of the twentieth century – and there were many – none so concerns biblical interpreters and Christian theologians as much as the Jewish *shoah* (Holocaust), a systematic genocide that sought to eradicate the Jewish people. That systematic assault on the Jewish community reduces serious theological thinkers to silence. Theodore Adorno has written, "To write poetry after Auschwitz is barbaric."[9] And Irving Greenberg has

---

[8] See Walter Brueggemann, "Reading from the Day 'In Between,'" in *A Shadow of Glory: Reading the New Testament after the Holocaust*, ed. Tod Linafelt (London: Routledge, 2002), 105–16.

[9] Theodore W. Adorno, *Prisms* (Cambridge, MA: MIT Press, 1981), 34.

concluded, "Let us offer, then, as a working principle the following: No statement, theological or otherwise, should be made that would not be credible in the presence of the burning children."[10] The *shoah* is indeed the abyss before which all theological explanation and interpretive conventions are reduced to silence. It is an abyss that is void of God and that exposes every theological claim to its thinness.

I do not suggest that the failure of Jerusalem in the sixth century BCE constitutes an abyss of the proportions of the twentieth-century *shoah*; Richard Rubenstein, for one, has denied any viable analogy between the two.[11] Having said that and taken it seriously, it is nonetheless the case that Jeremiah's rhetoric in the verbs of Jeremiah 1:10 provides a dramatic shape whereby this contemporary abyss of immense depth, extent, and viciousness can at least be framed in faith. There is another problem in the comparison, however, insofar as Jerusalem's crisis – informed by Deuteronomistic categories – is contained within the categories of culpability. But, in the end, Nebuchadnezzar is condemned as "out of control" and well beyond a calculus of punishment.[12] In other words, although culpability is a possible causation-explanation scenario, in the end it is neither satisfying nor correct; nor is such an explanation coterminous with the faith frame itself.

---

[10] Irving Greenberg, "Cloud of Smoke, Pillar of Fire," in *Holocaust: Religious and Philosophical Implications*, ed. John K. Roth and Michael Berenbaum (St. Paul, MN: Paragon House, 1989), 7–55.

[11] Richard L. Rubenstein, "Job and Auschwitz," *USQR* 25 (1970): 421–37.

[12] Of particular interest in this connection is the culmination of the poem in Lamentations 3. Israel's primary inclination is to accept sin as the cause of the destruction of Jerusalem. That note is sounded in Lamentations 3:42. As the poem develops, however, by verse 52 Israel is no longer the *perpetrator* but is now a *victim* of those who destroyed "without cause." The duality of perpetrator and victim continues in the exilic context.

Hence, the analogy between Jeremiah and the *shoah* is imprecise and inadequate. Even so, Jeremiah and his alert interpreters in the Book of Jeremiah knew in some depth the theological stress and problem that was to be enacted in the twentieth-century *shoah*. It can also be argued that the culpability argument is in the first instance not a theological point but a survivor's technique, a way of making sense out of lived nonsense.[13] Again, it is shown to be possible, but ultimately inadequate, as an explanation of theodicy.

Second, we may ponder the U.S. crisis of "9/11" caused by the "terrorist" assaults on the World Trade Center in New York and the Pentagon in Washington, D.C. Taken as an act of brutality, the 9/11 event is not overly spectacular because in the end it entailed a modest number of deaths. No doubt, that modest event has gained enormous symbolic importance because of its locus in New York City, a locus that invites perpetual media attention and commentary. Taken as a symbolic event, however, 9/11 is of enormous significance in U.S. culture, for it has introduced into U.S. awareness a dimension and depth of vulnerability that was heretofore unthinkable. Thus, that destruction, evoked to some extent by astonishingly imperialist posturing by the United States, alerted many people, particularly young people, to a world of risk not previously imagined among us. I submit that the loss of 9/11 is powerfully analogous to the loss of Jerusalem and its temple in 587 BCE. Both losses involve the exposure and jeopardy of the very

---

[13] Daniel L. Smith-Christopher, in his *A Biblical Theology of Exile*, OBT (Minneapolis: Fortress, 2002), has shown how the book of Ezekiel can be understood with reference to post-traumatic stress disorder. My colleague Kathleen O'Connor is now at work on the same sort of analysis with reference to the Book of Jeremiah. Thus the literature can be understood as a strategic effort at survival.

symbols generated by the community as a protection against such a threat. Furthermore, like the crisis of Jerusalem, 9/11, not unlike the *shoah*, does not easily respond to the categories of culpability. Thus, I propose that the tradition of Jeremiah is a powerful script in the contemporary context for giving dramatic articulation to the new vulnerability we face. The poetic utterance of Jeremiah, when transposed to 9/11, is not easily cast in the categories of cause and effect. More likely, the lines of prophetic utterance are available for probing, reflection, and haunting in the midst of a loss that cannot be readily contained in conventional modes of faith.

Third, if we take seriously the deep discontinuities of crucifixion, *shoah*, and 9/11 that defy conventional understandings, we may thus extrapolate in many directions to "lesser" abysses, the kind for which pastoral engagement is immediately appropriate. Such "minor abysses" are "minor" only if they happen to someone else. To everyone who experiences such an abyss, however, every such threat of destruction – a failed marriage, a lost love, a bad medical diagnosis, a pink slip, a disabling accident, and a thousand others – is as deep, ominous, and fearful as 587, the *shoah*, or 9/11.

In our eagerness to symbolize, we know that every such abyss must be "described" and then "redescribed" in rhetoric that is found to be adequate in its candor and in its *gravitas*. The Book of Jeremiah, for every such loss, is a script whereby crises are outlined and so made bearable if not ultimately containable. In the language of Paul Ricoeur, "limit experiences" that tax us with unbearable loss demand "limit expressions," so that the raw fact of life can be taken up into "meaning making."[14] Read in the ongoing arena of faith, the Book of Jeremiah is about every such abyss, later as well as original, personal as well as public. Every such loss requires the

---

[14] Paul Ricoeur, "Biblical Hermeneutics," *Semeia* 4 (1975): 107–45.

acknowledgment of what has in fact happened. Every such loss invites hope for newness beyond. Jeremiah as Scripture has not lingered over sixth-century BCE Jerusalem but has moved on apace, offering itself as a script for recurring deep losses and recurring wondrous newnesses.

Every person in a community who moves beyond *denial* in order to tell the truth and who defies *despair* in order to tell hope knows about the "crisis between."[15] The key issue, given destruction, is how newness can come. Even the Book of Jeremiah is not very clear on this expectation that admits of no clarity. But the Book of Jeremiah knows that at the bottom of the abyss there lingers the Lord of creation and the lover of Israel, in the midst of the decisive struggle that is required by sovereign indignation and compassionate fidelity. Only a poet has access to that hidden divine moment on which the future hangs. But the poet does have access – at least occasionally. That is why synagogues and churches cling to the tradition of Jeremiah. The Book of Jeremiah gives access to that "Saturday" moment in which the dread of Friday is overwhelmed in the newnesses of Easter.[16] All of that is known well, powerfully, and concretely in Jerusalem. In that script dwells the Holy One who in freedom brings to naught the things that are and in mercy calls into existence the things that are not (1 Cor 1:31; Rom 4:17).

---

[15] On the "between," see Alan E. Lewis, *Between Cross and Resurrection: A Theology of Holy Saturday* (Grand Rapids, MI: Eerdmans, 2001).

[16] See the remarkable statement of George Steiner concerning "Saturday" in his *Real Presences* (Chicago: University of Chicago Press, 1989), 231–32.

Further Reading

COMMENTARIES ON JEREMIAH

It is a remarkable happenstance of scholarship that until 1986 we had no full-length critical commentary in English on the Book of Jeremiah. Then, in 1986, Jeremiah studies were broken open in new ways with three important and superbly done commentaries. William L. Holladay, from a lifetime of work, offered the most complete historical-critical commentary that we are likely to have, treating the text conservatively and reading it for the most part as historically reliable. In the same year, from the extreme opposite perspective, Robert P. Carroll's commentary introduced "ideological critique" and for the most part rejected the historical claims of the text and called attention to the ideological factors in the theological claims of the text. It is fair to say that Carroll's commentary and approach, rather than that of Holladay, has exercised the most influence in setting interpretation in a quite new direction. In the same year, William McKane, faithful to the aims of the series in which his work appeared, presented a close study of textual issues in the Book of Jeremiah, with particular reference to the quite different Hebrew and Greek textual traditions. From these publications in 1986, Jeremiah studies have flourished for two decades, with a series of important and more accessible commentaries.

The more recent work includes the commentaries of John M. Bracke, Ronald E. Clements, Terence E. Fretheim, Patrick D. Miller, myself, and, most recently, Louis Stulman. For the most part, these commentaries move in the direction of theological interpretation, but the authors are well informed about the complexity of the Book of Jeremiah and take seriously the lingering verdict that the Book of Jeremiah is "unreadable." The important exception to this theological propensity is the three-volume work of Jack R. Lundbom, which is a foundational study in the tradition of Holladay. Because of the complexity of the text, these commentators are well aware that their best interpretive judgments are provisional. These commentaries reflect the remarkable ferment in Jeremian studies.

Bracke, John M. *Jeremiah 1–29*. Westminster Bible Companion. Louisville, KY: Westminster John Knox, 2000.

Jeremiah 30–52 and Lamentations. Westminster Bible Companion. Louisville, KY: Westminster John Knox, 2000.

Brueggemann, Walter. *A Commentary on Jeremiah: Exile and Homecoming*. Grand Rapids, MI: Eerdmans, 1998.

Carroll, Robert P. *Jeremiah: A Commentary*. Old Testament Library. Philadelphia: Westminster, 1986.

Clements, Ronald E. *Jeremiah*. Interpretation. Atlanta: John Knox, 1988.

Fretheim, Terence E. *Jeremiah*. Macon, GA: Smith and Helwys, 2002.

Holladay, William L. *Jeremiah 1: A Commentary on the Book of the Prophet Jeremiah Chapters 1–25*. Hermeneia. Philadelphia: Fortress, 1986.

Jeremiah 2: A Commentary on the Book of the Prophet Jeremiah Chapters 26–52. Hermeneia. Minneapolis: Fortress, 1989.

Lundbom, Jack R. *Jeremiah 1–20: A New Translation with Introduction and Commentary.* Anchor Bible 21 A. New York: Doubleday, 1999.

Jeremiah 21–36: A New Translation with Introduction and Commentary. Anchor Bible 21 B. New York: Doubleday, 2004.

Jeremiah 37–52: A New Translation with Introduction and Commentary. Anchor Bible 21 C. New York: Doubleday, 2004.

McKane, William. *A Critical and Exegetical Commentary on Jeremiah.* 2 vols. International Critical Commentary. Edinburgh: T. and T. Clark, 1986–1996.

Miller, Patrick D. "The Book of Jeremiah: Introduction, Commentary, and Reflections," in *The New Interpreter's Bible.* 12 vols. Ed. Leander Keck. Nashville, TN: Abingdon, 1994–. 6:553–926.

Stulman, Louis. *Jeremiah.* Abingdon Old Testament Commentaries. Nashville, TN: Abingdon, 2005.

STUDIES

The recent ferment in Jeremian studies is reflected in a plethora of journal articles and more expanded studies that concern both critical and hermeneutical issues. This list is representative of the important work that is under way in the field.

Anderson, Bernard W. "'The Lord Has Created Something New': A Stylistic Study of Jer 31:15–22." *Catholic Biblical Quarterly* 40 (1978): 463–77.

Bauer, Angela. *Gender in the Book of Jeremiah: A Feminist-Literary Reading.* New York: Peter Lang, 1999.

Baumgartner, Walter. *Jeremiah's Poems of Lament*. Sheffield:
    Almond, 1988 (German orig., 1917).
Childs, Brevard S. "The Enemy from the North and Chaos Tradi-
    tion." *Journal of Biblical Literature* 78 (1959): 187–98.
Dearman, J. Andrew. "'My Servants the Scribes': Composition
    and Context in Jeremiah 36." *Journal of Biblical Literature* 109
    (1990): 403–21.
Habel, Norman. "The Form and Significance of the Call Nar-
    ratives." *Zeitschrift für die alttestamentliche Wissenschaft* 77
    (1965): 297–323.
Kessler, Martin. "Jeremiah Chapters 26–45 Reconsidered." *Journal
    of Near Eastern Studies* 27 (1968): 81–88.
Perdue, Leo G. *The Collapse of History: Reconstructing Old Testa-
    ment Theology*. Overtures to Biblical Theology. Minneapolis:
    Fortress, 1994.
Perdue, Leo G. and Brian W. Kovacs, eds. *A Prophet to the Nations:
    Essays in Jeremiah Studies*. Winona Lake, IN: Eisenbrauns,
    1984.
Seitz, Christopher R. "The Prophet Moses and the Canonical Shape
    of Jeremiah." *Zeitschrift für die alttestamentliche Wissenschaft*
    101 (1989): 3–27.
Stulman, Louis. *The Prose Sermons of the Book of Jeremiah: A
    Redescription of the Correspondences with the Deuteronomistic
    Literature in the Light of Recent Text-Critical Research*. Society
    of Biblical Literature Dissertation Series 83. Atlanta: Scholars
    Press, 1986.
    "Insiders and Outsiders in the Book of Jeremiah: Shifts in Sym-
    bolic Arrangement." *Journal for the Study of the Old Testament*
    66 (1995): 65–85.
    Order Amid Chaos: Jeremiah as Symbolic Tapestry. The Biblical
    Seminar 57. Sheffield: Sheffield Academic Press, 1998.

THEOLOGY

The Book of Jeremiah, as difficult as it is critical, is a fertile and rich arena for interpretive activity. Perhaps the most generative study is that of Abraham J. Heschel, who moved quickly past critical questions to the "disclosure of God" in these texts. The other writings cited in this section participate in various ways in the radical disjunctions and extravagance of passion that are at the heart of faith in the Book of Jeremiah.

Carroll, Robert P. *From Chaos to Covenant: Prophecy in the Book of Jeremiah.* New York: Crossroad, 1981.

Diamond, A. R. *The Confessions of Jeremiah in Context: Scenes of Prophetic Drama.* Journal for the Study of the Old Testament Supplement Series 47. Sheffield: Sheffield Academic Press, 1987.

Diamond, A. R. Pete, Kathleen M. O'Connor, and Louis Stulman, eds. *Troubling Jeremiah.* Journal for the Study of the Old Testament Supplement Series 260. Sheffield: Sheffield Academic Press, 1999.

Heschel, Abraham J. *The Prophets.* New York: Harper and Row, 1962.

Nicholson, Ernest W. *Preaching to the Exiles: A Study of the Prose Tradition in the Book of Jeremiah.* Oxford: Blackwell, 1970.

O'Connor, Kathleen M. *The Confessions of Jeremiah: Their Interpretation and Their Role in Chapters 1–25.* Society of Biblical Literature Dissertation Series 94. Atlanta: Scholars Press, 1987.

Overholt, Thomas W. *The Threat of Falsehood: A Study in the Theology of the Book of Jeremiah.* Studies in Biblical Theology 16. London: SCM, 1970.

Smith, Mark S. *The Laments of Jeremiah and Their Contexts: A Literary and Redactional Study of Jeremiah 11–20*. Society of Biblical Literature Monograph Series 42. Atlanta: Scholars Press, 1990.

Recent literature on the Book of Jeremiah exhibits the way in which critical study of the book is moving away from older historical approaches to an emphasis on complex interpretive issues informed by more recent critical theory. This transition in method takes a variety of forms in a rich diversity of expressions. In times to come, special attention will no doubt be paid to the forthcoming work of Kathleen O'Connor that reads the Jeremian tradition through recent interpretive theory related to post-traumatic stress disorder.

Author Index

Scriptural Index